ANALYZING COSTS, PROCEDURES, PROCESSES, AND OUTCOMES IN HUMAN SERVICES

D1215845

Applied Social Research Methods Series
Volume 42

APPLIED SOCIAL RESEARCH METHODS SERIES

Series Editors
LEONARD BICKMAN, Peabody College, Vanderbilt University, Nashville
DEBRA J. ROG, Vanderbilt University, Washington, DC

Other volumes in this series are listed at the end of the book

ANALYZING COSTS, PROCEDURES, PROCESSES, AND OUTCOMES IN HUMAN SERVICES

Brian T. Yates

Applied Social Research Methods Series
Volume 42

SAGE Publications
International Educational and Professional Publisher
Thousand Oaks London New Delhi

For information address:

SAGE Publications, Inc.
2455 Teller Road
Thousand Oaks, California 91320
E-mail: order@sagepub.com

SAGE Publications Ltd.
6 Bonhill Street
London EC2A 4PU
United Kingdom

SAGE Publications India Pvt. Ltd.
M-32 Market
Greater Kailash I
New Delhi 110 048 India

Printed in the United States of America

Library of Congress Cataloging-in-Publication Data

Yates, Brian T.
    Analyzing costs, procedures, processes, and outcomes in human
services / author, Brian T. Yates.
        p.   cm.—(Applied social research methods; v. 42)
    Includes bibliographical references and index.
    ISBN 0-8039-4785-2 (acid-free paper).—ISBN 0-8039-4786-0 (pbk.:
acid-free paper)
        1. Human services—Evaluation—Methodology. 2. Human services—
Cost effectiveness. 3. Evaluation research (Social action
programs) 4. Present value analysis. I. Title. II. Series:
Applied social research methods series; v. 42.
HV11.Y37 1996
361'.0068'4—dc20   95-50211

This book is printed on acid-free paper.

96 97 98 99 00 01 10 9 8 7 6 5 4 3 2 1

Sage Production Editor: Gillian Dickens
Sage Typesetter: Andrea D. Swanson

Contents

I dedicate this book
to Bonnie and Robbie, my children,
and to Jan on this our 17th year of marriage.

Preface

Traditionally, cost-effectiveness analysis (CEA) and cost-benefit analysis (CBA) focus exclusively on comparisons of outcomes achieved by a service and the resources consumed by that service. CEA and CBA are complex procedures developed and refined by economists and management scientists. An extensive literature exists on the use of these techniques in business and educational settings (Kendall, 1971; Levine, 1983; Mishan, 1988; Peterson, 1986; Thompson, 1980). CEA and CBA also have been used in health and mental health settings (Davis & Frank, 1992; Weisbrod, 1983; Yates & Newman, 1980a, 1980b). This book introduces techniques for performing these traditional analyses in mental health and other human services, but it goes farther.

Because traditional cost-oriented analyses do not explain how one gets from a particular cost figure to a particular level of effectiveness or benefit, CEA and CBA by themselves do not reveal how services could be more cost-effective or cost-beneficial. CEA and CBA yield *summative* judgments—answers to the basic questions: How well does the program work and at what cost? How do the outcomes compare to the costs? These answers lead to additional questions: What is the most effective treatment for [a malady]? What is the least expensive way of providing this [most effective] treatment? These are the types of questions that begin to transform CEA and CBA into concrete strategies for optimizing programs. How to ask these sorts of *formative* evaluation questions is another focus of this book.

Finally, summative CEA and CBA and the formative versions of these analyses need to be melded so that the effects of the formative analyses are themselves evaluated. This integration orchestrates the summative and formative analyses and it also answers the question, Did this round of applied, clinical, and management research help the program deliver better or less expensive services? Or more generally, Was this evaluation-improvement cycle worth *its* cost? The relation between evaluation and other forms of social science research is the overarching theme of this book, as it is of the Applied Social Research Methods Series to which this book belongs.

The first chapter describes a model for comprehensive assessment and improvement-oriented analysis of human service systems. This model brings traditional CEA and CBA methods to bear on the research, evaluation, and management concerns of social scientists and program evaluators. Each subsequent chapter includes methods for and examples of analyzing each of the links between the expenditure of resources and the achievement of long-term program objectives. Examples of each step in understanding and improving relationships between resources used, processes enacted, and outcomes produced are drawn from the author's evaluation research in residential and outpatient substance abuse programs, nonprofit mental health clinics, inpatient treatments for schizophrenics, residential programs for dependent or neglected urban youth, intermediate care facilities for mentally retarded adults, obesity treatments, suicide prevention programs, self-management training, and mental health programs for children of homeless families. The examples are designed to encourage readers to explore the concepts and techniques of the chapter by conducting their own quantitative and qualitative analyses of cost → procedure → process → outcome paths in human services.

Acknowledgments

Many people helped make this book possible; there's space here to mention only a few. Fred Newman has inspired and encouraged me for many years. I doubt that I would have persevered without his support; he has been there right when I needed him most. Jim Filipczak has been a colleague in many settings since the late 1970s; he has provided many opportunities to test and develop the ideas in this book. More recently, Karst Besteman has provided additional wisdom and further opportunities to refine my model for cost $\to$ procedure $\to$ process $\to$ outcome analysis as did Margaret Camarena even more recently. Karst's faith in the importance of assessing costs as well as outcomes helped me maintain confidence in the importance of my work. Margaret made clear to me the relevance of the CPPOA model to prevention as well as to treatment. Several anonymous reviewers helped improve this manuscript markedly. Last, I thank Len Bickman and Debra Rog for their professional help in refining the manuscript and for their patience and persistence in seeing this manuscript from inspiration through publication.

1

The Scientist-Manager-Practitioner and Cost → Procedure → Process → Outcome Analysis

THE ORGANIZATION OF THIS BOOK

A new role has emerged in the field of social services: a highly educated professional who already has dual training as a practitioner and as a social scientist but who is asked to develop a third area of expertise—the management of social service systems. This three-in-one role demands a new conceptualization of human services—one that formally recognizes elements of the service system that are the foci of managerial *and* clinical *and* scientific efforts. This book provides a new approach to the management of human services that integrates clinical and experimental strategies in ways that may help the scientist-manager-practitioner (SMP). More specifically, the following chapters present a framework for evaluating, managing, and systematically improving the outcomes of mental health and other human service systems by:

- selecting those *resources* needed to
- implement the mixture of *procedures* that
- encourage social, psychological, and perhaps other *processes* that, in turn,
- produce those changes in behaviors, thoughts, and feelings that are the desired short-term and long-term *outcomes* of the service.

The present chapter describes the SMP role and offers a model of service systems for the SMP, for program evaluators, and for students of program evaluation and human services administration. Chapter 2 illustrates basic methods of measuring the costs of human service programs. Chapter 3 provides concepts and strategies for studying relationships between the overt procedures and the numerous covert processes involved in the provision of human services. Measuring effectiveness and benefits—outcomes—is the focus of Chapter 4. Chapter 5 explains how to put together cost, procedure, process, and outcome information to more completely describe, better understand, and best improve the cost-effectiveness and cost-benefit of human services.

GOALS OF THE SCIENTIST-MANAGER-PRACTITIONER

The SMP has these goals:

- To continually improve the delivery of human services
- To manage human service systems in an empirically accountable manner
- To respond assertively and empirically to questions about effectiveness, benefit, cost-effectiveness, and cost-benefit
- To advance understanding of the origins, treatment, and prevention of psychological, social, and physical dysfunction

To Continually Improve the Delivery of Human Services

"Improving the delivery of human services" means different things to different interest groups. The SMP role typically encompasses multiple interest group perspectives, because no one perspective yields a complete picture of what is going on in the service system. Comprehensive models of the service system offer the best chance of finding effective solutions to problems in delivering services. Improving the delivery of human services has been used to mean providing more services, providing better services, providing less expensive services, or providing the same services to more people. Perhaps a less ambiguous and more succinct statement of this SMP goal is this: *to provide the best to the most for the least.*

This is a challenging goal; only after several cycles of program evaluation, manipulation, and reevaluation can it hope to be approximated. Technically, one can either optimize outcome within budget constraints or minimize the costs of achieving a particular set of outcomes. Successive iterations of formative evaluation can approach the goal of delivering "the best to the most for the least" by finding out which cost constraints could be slackened with maximum improvement in outcome and then, which outcome criteria could be loosened with maximum reduction in cost (Eck, 1976, chap. 7; Hillier & Lieberman, 1974).

The Best. This generally means services that can be expected, on the basis of prior clinical experience and research, to be the most effective in the long run. A different definition of *best* is used when one method of delivering services is said to be better than others because it is more expensive or in closer adherence to standard or ideal service characteristics. Often, the same service (e.g., treatment for heroin addiction) can be delivered in alternative ways (e.g., residential or outpatient, drug-free or methadone maintenance). Higher quality of this sort does not always produce better outcomes. The *best* is used here to describe a service that is constituted and delivered in a manner that can be expected to maximize effectiveness or to at least meet high criteria for program outcomes.

To the Most. The best human service is worthless if it cannot be offered to the people who need it. Ideally, a human service system maintains a high level of effectiveness while serving the entire population of individuals who need the service. Given limited public funding and scarce private resources for most human services, and given the limited ability of our service techniques to improve clients' lives, only a proportion of the population in need can be truly helped by most services. Nevertheless, most human service providers wish to serve the highest possible proportion of those in need while maintaining a highly effective service. There is, of course, the option of diminishing the effectiveness of the service so that it can be offered to more individuals. This "spread thinner but broader" strategy is not what most SMPs would advocate as a goal, even though it all too often is our reality.

For the Least. In part, the desire to minimize the expense of a human service is a result of wishing to serve the largest number of people in need. Given a fixed budget and a set level of service, the less it costs to serve each individual, the larger the number of individuals that can be served. In addition, some human service providers feel morally obligated to consume no more of the limited resources of society than is necessary. This impetus to conserve societal resources allows other human services to reach more individuals in need of those services. By avoiding excessive consumption of society's wealth, SMPs show respect for the economic ecology of the human service sector. SMPs who control costs even can prevent some additions to client rosters that may result from additional taxation that might lead to lower economic growth and higher unemployment.

To Manage Human Service Systems
in an Empirically Accountable Manner

Running a clinic, hospital, agency, or other service system can be so demanding and hectic an endeavor that the last thing one has time for is to keep track of the number of clients seen and the types of service rendered. Requests to report regularly on the services delivered can be construed as impositions that require time one does not have and that represent doubts about motives and capabilities that one certainly *does* have. Nevertheless, most professionals acknowledge the importance of being able to describe to funders, to client advocates, and to the public in general the magnitude and manner of services provided. Some providers view the provision of human services as a public trust for which one is bound to maintain basic records of who received what services when. Other providers are made to feel responsible to funders and others who request regular reports on the quality and quantity of services delivered. Whatever the reason, it now is generally accepted that human services must be accountable for the resources they consume (i.e., their costs), for the services they provide, and for the outcomes they produce.

To Respond Assertively and Empirically to Questions About Effectiveness, Benefit, Cost-Effectiveness, and Cost-Benefit

Numbers speak louder than words at times and can help resolve questions about the cost, quality, or outcomes of human services. Being able to state the average cost of each episode of client contact and to report quantitative indices of the quality and results of services can invite criticism, too. One may hear, for example, "Why does it cost so much?" and "Why doesn't everyone get better?" Empirical evidence that a service has indeed been provided and that some positive outcomes were found for some clients can be strong defenses against attacks such as, "They're just picking up their paychecks at the end of the month" and "Nobody gets any help from them anyway, so why not cut their budget?"

The best defense against criticisms of cost, service quality, or effectiveness probably is an efficient operation that accomplishes the most with the least. Many service systems can benefit from regular internal reports on the amounts of services delivered, their costs, and their short-term and long-term outcomes. Routine feedback of data on costs, therapeutic procedures, and outcomes can reinforce components of the service system that work well and can draw attention to areas that need improvement.

To Advance Understanding of the Origins, Treatment, and Prevention of Psychological, Social, and Physical Dysfunction

Some providers and some administrators of human services have little hope that theory and research will help services become more effective.

Instead, they say, we simply need more money to provide more of the services that we know will work if provided in sufficient quantities to enough people. That certainly may be so. It also is possible that addressing the problems of individuals one at a time is the wrong way to help. Fundamental changes may be needed in the systems that teach, rear, train, pay, tax, and judge people. Therapy for spouse abusers, for example, may be a small and temporary bandage on a problem rooted in deeper social and economic issues.

Prevention of human problems is an alternative to traditional clinical treatment that could save years of suffering, improve the quality and duration of many lives, and free public and private funds for investment elsewhere. Because they operate prior to (and ideally in lieu of) occurrence of the actual problem, prevention efforts rely very much on theory to guide them. Research offers a widely supported way in which to develop, validate, and compare theories of the origins of human problems and how they can best be avoided. In particular, it is possible that significant human and social problems can be prevented by helping individuals recover from traumas and by educating groups to the risks they take when engaging in certain behaviors. Also, cycles of abuse, neglect, and aggression that perpetuate mental and social ills may be ended by therapy that helps individuals escape from repetition of behaviors that could be destructive to themselves and others.

It has long been recognized that not all prevention efforts and programs work, however, and that not all services work equally well for everybody. Which methods work best for which types of clients when provided by which professionals in what communities are questions that, if answered, might aid achievement of the goal of delivering the best to the most for the least. Research provides a systematic way of finding concrete answers to these questions.

Conducting this sort of clinical research would be easy if reliable and valid data already were reported on outcomes, on the types and amounts of therapy provided, on the resources required to provide those therapy services, and on details such as client and therapist characteristics. Collecting and reporting this information regularly is difficult, however, especially when program funds are limited. Nevertheless, a service system that does gather this information regularly in the interests of accountability and better management can understand better how it can make itself as effective as possible with as few resources as necessary. This general approach, except for the collection of cost information, has been advocated for individual scientist-practitioners (e.g., DeMuth, Yates, & Coates, 1984; Gottman & Leiblum, 1974; Kazdin, 1993). This book is devoted to explaining how this sort of clinical research can be performed for entire human service systems. In addition, this book describes methods of defining and collecting information on the costs, effectiveness, benefits, and methods of human services. Measuring the important variables is crucial: A variable unmeasured has little influence on quantitative decisions. The quality of the information collected on costs, outcomes, and service methods is crucial, too: Low quality data make for a low quality model, which can in turn support disastrous decisions.

A MODEL FOR HUMAN SERVICE SYSTEMS: COST → PROCEDURE → PROCESS → OUTCOME ANALYSIS (CPPOA)

To achieve the goals of the SMP, it is useful to conceptualize human service systems in a manner that guides the collection and analysis of information from many sources. Many models and theories of service program design and functioning are available (Bickman, 1987; Bickman, Hedrick, & Rog, 1993; Chen, 1990; Guba & Lincoln, 1989; Kuhn, 1974; Rog, 1985; Rossi & Chen, 1992). In general, examining only the inputs and outputs of service systems does not produce the level of understanding needed to conduct a meaningful evaluation (Lipsey, 1993) or to optimize cost-effectiveness or cost-benefit. In mental health and social services especially, relationships between funds input, outcomes observed, and intervening acts and events do not always adhere to what is normal, expected, or common sense (Yates, 1994). The resulting model of a human service system should encompass the therapeutic efforts that are enabled by the system, the outcomes of those efforts, and the expenditures that make possible the delivery of therapeutic services. In addition, the model should clearly state what the critical service procedures are. A complete model should specify the psychological, biological, social, and other processes inside the client that are supposed to be changed by service procedures. Finally, the model should provide a framework for reporting and improving outcomes and costs.

The CPPOA model diagrammed in Table 1.1 conceptualizes human services as systems that select and consume a variety of resources for the purpose of implementing components of a treatment program (Yates, 1995). These program procedures are designed to cause changes in clients' behaviors, cognitions (thoughts), and affects (emotions) via changes within the clients. The effect of treatment procedures on these psychological and

Table 1.1

Examples of Resource → Procedure → Process → Outcome Relationships in Human Services

Resources →	Program Procedures →	Psychosocial Processes →	Other Processes Related to the Following: →	Interim Outcomes →	Long-Term Outcomes
Temporal	Individual counseling	Skill acquisition	Client characteristics	Relations with . . .	Continuation of
Direct service	Psychological	Self-control	Age	Peers	interim outcomes
Paid	Medical	Social	Gender	Children	Cost savings in:
Volunteer	Group counseling	Job seeking	Race	Spouse or mate	Health services
Administrative	Women's	Vocational	Prior treatment	Relatives	Mental health
Other indirect	Men's	Relapse prevention	Employment	Employer	services
Management	Prevocational	Expectancies	Physically	Others	Welfare
Information	Relapse prevention	Self-efficacy	challenged	Employment	Employee
System	Education	Outcome	Medical	Independent living	assistance
Material	Drug abuse	Compliance	complications	Cessation of	program
Equipment	Health and	Difficulty of	Psychological	substance abuse	operation
Direct service	nutrition	treatment	complications	Preferred drug	Training of new
Administrative	Referrals	Relationships and	Therapist	Other drugs	employees
Supplies	Health	social support	characteristics	HIV transmission	Benefits accrued:
Medicines	Social services	Therapist	Training	behaviors	Tax revenues
Psychometric	Legal aid	Family	Experience	Physical health	Positive modeling
tests	Vocational	Peers	History	Mental health	for others
Office supplies	Extraprogram	Employers	Age		(prevention)
Spatial		Spouse or mate	Gender		Improved family
Direct service		Others	Race		and social
Administrative			Addiction physiology		climate
Other indirect					
Transportation					
Communications					
Financing					

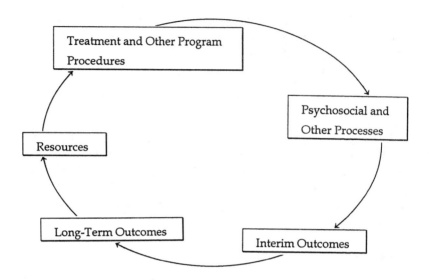

Figure 1.1. Possible Cyclic Relationship Between Resources, Procedures, Processes, and Outcomes

biological processes may be mediated by interactions with client characteristics, client biology, the culture of the client, therapist characteristics, and other variables.

The results of these processes and interactions should, in turn, lead to interim outcomes, such as decreased substance abuse, enhanced personal regard, or better functioning in several spheres such as family life and employment. The long-term outcomes of substance abuse treatment involve benefits to society such as productive labor and tax revenues as well as savings in health care expenses and in other service resources that otherwise would have to be spent. Anticipation of these social benefits may motivate funders to allocate scarce resources to human services. The degree to which society actually benefits from human services may determine the amount of resources subsequently allocated to the human services, closing the circle of relationships between resources, process, procedures, and outcomes (see Figure 1.1).

Before measuring the amount of resources used to implement program processes that produce particular outcomes, we first need to understand what those costs, procedures, processes, and outcomes are. Definitions of these elements of the CPPOA model follow. Subsequent chapters provide more detailed definitions of each system component along with methods of developing a qualitative and quantitative understanding of each element as it interacts with others in the provision of human services.

COSTS (RESOURCES CONSUMED)

Decisions about which resources to include in cost assessment and how to assess their value are largely a function of the interest group perspective, as discussed in the next chapter. The following paragraphs describe comprehensive assessment of all resources used in the treatment endeavor; less all-encompassing cost assessments are possible and can be useful for certain decisions.

Personnel

The time and services of people are the most expensive and essential resources consumed by human services. These resources can be quantified in different ways. Salaries plus medical and other benefits, incentive payments, and consulting fees all provide a monetary estimate of the value of these resources. If substantial volunteered time is involved or if pay varies according to criteria other than the quality of service provided (e.g., strictly according to seniority), the value of personnel resources may be better estimated according to the amount of time spent by each person in service-related activities.

Whether time or money is used as the unit by which the value of personnel resources is measured, the amount of time or finances devoted to implementation of each major treatment procedure needs to be recorded or estimated for each episode of service to each client. Only by isolating the value of resources spent per client can we later investigate quantitatively the relationships between costs (i.e., resource expenditures) and procedures, processes, and outcomes.

In recognition of the higher value that society places on particular staff members' (e.g., physicians') time, one can place a final value on the personnel resources devoted to a particular client by multiplying the hours spent by each staff member by their rate of pay. For salaried personnel, the rate of pay is calculated by dividing their annual salary by the number of days that they are expected to work in a year. Volunteered time can be valued by multiplying the number of hours spent in direct or indirect service activities by the rate of pay they would receive for their services elsewhere. The value of time volunteered by professionals may be assessed according to the rate of pay they would receive in their professional activities. For example, a physician who volunteers to counsel clients about emotional problems can have his or her time valued according to the rate of pay as a physician rather than as a counselor. This evaluation method is one of several available.

Administrative and other staff not delivering direct services generally should have their time divided among clients in proportion to the time that direct service staff devotes to the specific clients. Indirect service staff include, in many service systems, directors, business managers, accountants, consultants, management information system specialists, administrative assistants, and receptionists.

Facilities, Utilities

Although human services are labor intensive almost by definition (which makes personnel the largest item in budgets and the major resource to assess), offices and other space devoted to treatment also are part of any comprehensive model of a service system. The amount of space (e.g., square meters) devoted to treatment of a particular client can be measured in *square-meter hours* or similar units. The value of square-meter hours is determined by dividing the lease, rental, or other monetary cost of the space used by the number of square meters in each particular area and then by the total number of hours of service delivery received by all clients. Utilities and furniture rental or purchase expenses are proportioned among clients according to their square-meter hours, as are janitorial services and other maintenance expenses.

Equipment

The value of computers, biofeedback apparatus, and other equipment used by human service systems is proportioned among clients according to the hours of service they receive. Clients who do not receive a treatment procedure that uses a particular piece of equipment would not have a portion of the value of that apparatus included in their cost assessment. For example, former substance abusers who are no longer receiving methadone but who are receiving counseling to help them remain drug free would not have included in their figurative bill the expense of pumps for daily dispensing of methadone, nurse and physician contact time, and equipment for mixing methadone solutions. The monetary value of equipment can be estimated on a daily or hourly basis according to depreciation rates appropriate for that apparatus. Equipment not involved in direct services (e.g., phones, fax machines, and computer hardware and software) still can be valued according to depreciation rates and can be assigned to clients in proportion to the amount of direct services received by each client. Donated equipment can be valued in the same way as if it had been purchased, to provide a complete and accurate model of resources used in treatment.

Supplies, Pharmacological Agents

The cost of consumables such as methadone and the cup into which it is dispensed are included in direct treatment costs along with psychological tests, medical supplies, and other materials used in direct services. The monetary value of office supplies, such as computer and fax paper, file folders, and forms, usually are distributed among clients according to the hours of direct service they receive.

PROCEDURES ENACTED

These are the actual procedures that constitute the delivery of treatment or other services. They are concrete and observable events, such as counseling sessions or an appointment with a physician. Accreditation of service sites and continued funding of service systems often are contingent on satisfactory assessments of the degree to which planned treatment procedures actually are implemented. The quality of treatment procedure implementation can include the frequency with which particular topics are addressed in sessions or whether training sessions for particular skills have been held. These procedure evaluations do not focus on results of the procedures, such as whether the skill actually was acquired by the client. The actual acquisition of a skill would be a process rather than a procedure, as would the use of that skill. The procedure evaluation would ask whether the treatment service combined the necessary resources to provide the opportunity for the client to acquire the skill.

Service system procedures can include the following:

- Group counseling (e.g., unemployment support groups, relapse prevention)
- Educational meetings (e.g., nutrition, relaxation training)
- Individual counseling (e.g., short-term psychotherapy, cognitive-behavioral therapy)

- Medical services (e.g., immunization for influenza, diagnosis and treatment of sexually transmitted diseases)
- Other services (e.g., psychological testing, neurological assessment)
- Referrals (e.g., for health, social, legal, and vocational services)

To be able to analyze more accurately and completely the contribution of service procedures to changes in client functioning and other interim and long-term outcomes, one can attempt to monitor services that clients receive outside of the service system. Extraprogram services may be important additional procedures that contribute to outcomes independent of, or in positive interaction with, the procedures used in the system under study. In drug abuse treatment, extraprogram treatment procedures may include meetings of Narcotics Anonymous, Alcoholics Anonymous, and posttreatment residential programs, such as the Oxford House program. In recovery from coronary heart disease, extraprogram procedures might include courses in meditation, martial arts, smoking cessation, or nutrition. Informal activities (e.g., recreational outings) are procedures that may contribute to outcomes and thus are additional treatment procedures to monitor.

PROCESSES CREATED OR
ENHANCED BY PROCEDURES

Psychological and Social Processes

The particular procedures that are chosen for implementation in a service system often owe their existence to tradition as well as to specific expectancies that the procedures will set into motion *processes* involving the cognitions and emotions of the client. Processes differ from procedures in that processes usually occur *within the skin* of the individual who has been targeted as the client, whereas *procedures* are observable actions of professionals and others who are trying to help the client. The holding of an encounter group is a procedure, but changes produced by that procedure in clients' feelings and self-concepts are processes. Similarly, if a community is the client, a community mobilization effort involving flyers and meetings might be procedures that would foster increased awareness of threats to the community, increased community identity, and increased empowerment (Alinsky, 1971). Many a workshop, training session, and retreat are procedures used by businesses in attempts to improve and direct organizational processes, such as focus, consensus, and efficiency.

Processes might be best grouped under the label *psychological,* although they can be more social, economic, or physical. Also, the exact processes targeted may vary according to the theoretical inclination of the service provider or planner. The treatment procedure of individual counseling can, for example, be designed to either remove barriers to clients' understanding of the nature of their problems, improve self-efficacy, uncover and release enduring anger and guilt, or guide the clients toward better self-management. Psychological processes commonly evoked by human service procedures include the following:

- Realization and understanding of origins and maintaining conditions (e.g., awareness of why a pattern of self-defeating cognitions and emotions began; why the client allows it to continue; and what social, environmental, and economic factors encourage this)
- Skill acquisition (e.g., job résumé preparation, interviewing, assertiveness training, anxiety management)
- Expectancies (e.g., expectations that infection will not occur if condoms are used, self-efficacy expectancies for successful parenting)
- Relationships (e.g., trusting one's therapist, stable relationships with one's mate) and many other mediating processes

Other Processes

The literature on treatment outcomes has included speculation that the effects of treatment procedures are mediated by social and biological processes set in motion when a particular client begins counseling with a particular therapist. In addition to these processes, others may interact with the psychological processes to determine outcomes:

- Therapist characteristics (e.g., whether the therapist has been addicted to a substance in the past and whether that substance was alcohol, another drug, or multiple substances, plus the therapist's age, gender, ethnic group, training, degree, and demographic and socioeconomic similarity to the client)
- Client characteristics (e.g., the length and severity of addiction; number of substances addicted to; number as well as duration and success of previous treatments for substance abuse; client's age, gender, ethnic group, employment status; and the existence of medical complications, severe mental health dysfunction, personality disorders, physical handicaps, and other forms of dual or multiple diagnoses)
- Health and physiology (e.g., metabolic rate, immune system functioning, addiction; certain treatment procedures may produce changes in self-

efficacy expectancies that can help clients control moderate addiction to alcohol)

- Social support (e.g., the existence and strength of family and peer support systems that encourage completion of high school and college; groups may foster peer pressure to excel academically as well as socially)

Naturally, more processes could be considered: These will vary according to the program, community, provider, and client. It seems likely that what is done in and by the service system and by clients outside of the service system are not the sole determinants of outcomes. One can imagine several ways in which socioeconomic and political processes beyond the control of the client or service system could enhance or detract from the effectiveness of treatment. Client outcomes may not be as positive, for example, if even the best-equipped high school dropout seeks employment during a persistent recession. Treatment procedures could be impeded when economic and political conditions prompt severe reductions in the quality and quantity of services provided. Although these last processes cannot be manipulated by those responsible for providing treatment, they may be important to consider when attempting to understand the strength of relationships between resources, procedures, targeted processes, and outcomes.

INTERIM (PROXIMAL) OUTCOMES PRODUCED

It is tempting, and traditional, to consider outcomes to be what happens after treatment stops. An alternative view is that outcomes of treatment can start occurring as soon as those processes are in effect. These proximal or *interim outcomes* differ from processes in that processes occur within individuals—inside the skin, as it were—whereas interim outcomes are the observable results of processes.

Interim outcomes that occur during treatment include changes in:

- Clients' overall functioning
- Drug abuse
- Maladaptive behavior (e.g., criminal behavior to gain entry to a gang, white-collar crime that facilitates acceptance into an "inner circle")
- Employment and related activities (e.g., interviews, employment-related education, employment, and performance on the job)

- Independent living (e.g., housing status, food availability, clothing, personal hygiene, socially appropriate behavior when in public)
- Reduction in HIV transmission behaviors (e.g., use of condoms, reduction in the number of sexual partners, engagement in lower risk forms of sexual interaction)
- Physical health (e.g., nutrition, fitness, immunocompetence, cardiovascular functioning, psychosomatic symptoms)
- Mental health (e.g., self-regard, depression, anxiety)
- Adoption of more positive personal values, life goals, and lifestyle (e.g., orientation toward nurturing others, personal growth)
- Pursuit of education (e.g., studying for a high school equivalency degree, a part-time or full-time return to college or graduate school, vocational courses, continuing education)
- Transfer of outcomes to others' lives (e.g., changes in the mental, physical, and social functioning of coworkers, fellow clients, family, spouses, or mates that can be attributed, in part, to changes in the life of the client)

LONG-TERM (DISTAL) OUTCOMES YIELDED

Interim outcomes are monitored closely by most service providers so that treatment procedures can be adjusted for unforeseen interactions with other procedures to obtain the best short-term effects possible. Long-term outcomes include maintenance of, if not continued improvement in, the interim outcomes. In addition, long-term outcomes include the benefits that accrue to society when interim outcomes are produced and maintained for substantial numbers of people over considerable periods of time. These benefits often can be valued in monetary units after initially measuring them in terms of occurrence rates or frequency.

Contributions to Society

Successfully treated clients may become more effective members of society; they may work more and pay more taxes. Succinctly put, someone who is functioning at a higher level should be able to take better care of themselves and help others. Successfully served clients also may be even more likely than other people to volunteer some of their time to work with substance abusers or those who are otherwise disadvantaged. Some of these contributions can be measured by the salary a client earns and the amount of taxes they pay to various governments through sundry expenditures, payroll deductions, and income tax payments. Volunteered time and services can be valued with procedures described earlier, although these may not capture the importance of volunteering time for either the persons being helped or for the former clients themselves.

It is, of course, possible that some services will achieve positive outcomes for clients while actually diminishing the client's apparent, immediate contribution to society. Transforming a Type A survivor of a heart attack into a Type B person may diminish the number of hours the client will work and the number of projects they will take on. Nevertheless, the long-term contributions of this client to his or her employer and to family and friends may amount to more than would have accrued if they had not reduced their risk of future, and possibly fatal, heart attacks.

Reduced Use of Medical and Social Services

A successfully treated client will continue to use certain human services but probably will no longer need to be the focus of intensive treatment procedures. If the client were not treated successfully, it seems likely that treatment would continue or other services would be used at some time in the future. The degree to which this is the case can be measured with control groups of clients who, through random assignment to waiting lists or self-selection, were not exposed to treatment procedures at the same time as the clients being monitored in the evaluation. The costs of services used by control clients but not by treated clients may be considerable, as may be the reduction in service expense for treated clients.

Reduced Criminal Activity and
Reduced Criminal Justice Services

In addition to reduced use of social and treatment services, one might expect a reduction in criminal activities and in criminal justice services for those clients who previously had engaged in illegal activities. Investigation, apprehension, adjudication, incarceration, and probation all are relatively expensive services. Any reduction in these could amount to significant cost savings to society, making reduced criminal service use a monetary benefit to include in comparisons of costs versus benefits of providing a human service. Furthermore, reduced criminal activity may more directly realize a considerable savings to society via reduced assaults (assessed as reductions in those medical and therapy expenses that are associated with being assaulted) and by reduced theft (e.g., valued as the costs of replacing stolen pension funding plus possible changes in insurance rates and provision of additional security precautions in computer networks as a result of the theft).

Improved Social Climate

Although this type of long-term outcome may be perceived as the most subjective and vacuous of those listed, it may yield the biggest social effect. Consider, for example, that each person in the community who is not abusing drugs may act as a positive model for other persons who are at risk for initiation of, or relapse to, drug use. As more persons cease drug use and adopt a drug-free lifestyle, a culture counter to that which encourages drug abuse is more likely to emerge as a powerful determinant of individual behavior. This sort of community-level change may seem unlikely at current rates of treatment success and funding. If treatment procedures are adequately funded, however, and are successful with a sufficient number of substance-abusing clients, it is remotely possible that the milieu of inner cities and suburbs would change so that large-scale enterprises for the import and distribution of illegal drugs would no longer be viable. This could be a sizable social benefit that, due to its complexity and vastness, would be a challenge to measure and monetize completely and accurately. Other interventions, such as for smoking cessation, might more readily be shown to have this magnitude of effect on the community gestalt.

Development of New Treatment Techniques

More likely than the enhancement of an entire community's social climate, at least for now, is the production of modified or entirely new treatment techniques. These techniques would use the same amount or types of personnel, facilities, and other resources but achieve greater effect (i.e., superior interim and long-term outcomes). The value of these techniques, should they be developed, could be assessed and compared to traditional techniques in terms of outcomes and costs.

ANALYZING COMPONENTS
OF CPPOA MODELS

So far, the building blocks of a comprehensive human service system model have been described, and methods of assigning numbers to each have been alluded to. A model does little to help provide better human services, however, if it is not analyzed (i.e., *used*).

Describing Costs, Procedures, Processes, and Outcomes

Even the initial steps in developing a CPPOA model of the system model can, by themselves, instigate improvements in the functioning of that system. Construction of the CPPOA model externalizes administrators', clinicians', clients', and funders' understanding of what is being done to what aspects of the client using what resources, all for the purpose of producing what outcomes. This may be the first time that all major players in system operations have discussed or shared an understanding of what is going on and why. The disagreements that are a natural part of generating a model can be constructive in that they make explicit the different perspectives of service consumers, producers, and investors and can educate all parties concerned. Indeed, these and related processes prepare an organization for quantitative evaluation. How the organization responds to this initial step in CPPOA may predict how valuable it is (Rog, 1985; Wholey, 1983, 1987a, 1987b). Furthermore, by depicting the service system as a series of operations, participants can consider various ways of achieving the desired outcomes. New treatment procedures can be proposed by redrawing parts of the diagram. The use of different resources and the targeting of different psychological processes and outcomes also can be depicted easily using this sort of qualitative model.

The addition of quantitative information to this qualitative model can enrich it with increased concreteness and superior malleability. By specifying the particular resources being used (e.g., the amount of volunteered time used in a crisis intervention program and the amount of time spent by clinical staff in the same effort), the SMP and other parties gain understandings of why program services have particular costs. Similarly, increased understanding of a current service system is likely after specific procedures, processes, and interim and long-term outcomes are defined, operationalized, measured, and reported. Methods described in subsequent chapters show how these quantification descriptions can be made palatable to persons who normally turn quickly past pages with numeric expressions.

Understanding Relationships Between Costs, Procedures, Processes, and Outcomes

The next challenge in analyzing a model of a service system is depicting the relationships between different elements of the model (e.g., between resources and treatment procedures). The qualitative parts of the CPPOA service system model describe the existence and direction of relationships with lines and arrows between resources and procedures, procedures and processes, processes and interim outcomes, and interim and long-term outcomes (Yates, 1995). The quantitative portions of the same model assign numeric values to the relationships. The strength of each relationship can be indicated by the width of the line between, say, a particular resource and a certain treatment procedure.

If data are obtained via a traditional research design, analysis of variance and related statistics can be applied to compare differences in outcomes. If a more detailed and comprehensive approach to measurement has been taken, however, analyses can examine relationships between each part of the model. These analyses would begin by using correlations and multiple regressions to assess both the strength and direction of relationships between resources expended and program procedures enacted. The next analyses would investigate how the processes induced by service procedures may be related to psychological processes that occur or continue, following cessation of the service. These investigations can provide the basis for further analyses that would measure the strength of various paths between (a) the amounts of particular resources consumed, (b) the degrees to which treatment procedures are enacted, (c) the reliability with which these procedures engender specific processes, and (d) the extents to which desired interim and long-term outcomes are achieved.

Using the Findings of CPPOA

Once the strengths of relationships between resources, procedures, processes, and outcomes have been measured, quantitative descriptions of these relationships can be manipulated mathematically. These CPPOAs can amount to simple correlations between procedures (receiving or not receiving job training, for example) and outcomes (e.g., employment status and income over the next 4 years). CPPOA can, however, be more than this. To help the SMPs achieve their mission, CPPOA can use optimization functions available in common spreadsheet software (e.g., Microsoft's Excel) or specialized business programs (e.g., Chan & Sullivan, 1986) to discover how outcomes can be maximized within the cost constraints of the service system by varying the degree to which different treatment procedures are implemented. The more efficient procedures typically are retained and implemented to a greater degree, whereas the less efficient or more costly procedures are implemented to a lesser degree or not at all. In large service systems that have the responsibility to treat a variety of clients, separate analyses may be needed to determine how to maximize the effectiveness of treatment within budget constraints for each

clientele separately. Treatment resources, procedures, processes, and outcomes might be discernibly different, for instance, for the drug abuser than
for the well-functioning "casual" user, or for the unemployed mother-to-be
as opposed to a working woman.

Higher-order analyses then will need to consider what mixture of services to provide so as to not exceed total program resources while maximizing the number of clients who obtain outcomes that meet basic criteria.
Even more global analyses could be conducted to maximize the number of
clients obtaining desired outcomes from different social services, for
example, mental health versus education.

Limitations of CPPOA

Naturally, the findings of CPPOA are not the sole, or necessarily the
principal, determinant of which treatment components are retained and increased and which are diminished or discarded. Office politics, requirements
from constituents or providers to include certain components regardless of
their effectiveness or cost, and other matters can play significant roles in
decision making in any organization—and certainly in human service systems.
More than the findings of most CPPOAs, political and economic considerations will be likely to determine the allocation of resources among different
clinics and different social endeavors. Helping decision makers understand the
findings of CPPOA is important: Communicating the findings and their
implications for cost allocation and outcome attainment can be a challenge.

Appreciating and properly representing the limitations of CPPOA findings
is similarly important. Measurement of costs, procedures, processes, and
outcomes always will be imperfect. There will be random and systematic
biases in some of the data obtained. The relationships depicted by CPPOA also
may be in error in some cases, due to problems with the initial measures or the
ways in which they were analyzed. There may be more wisdom than is initially
appreciated in decision makers' habit of using, but not revering, the recommendations generated by any quantitative or qualitative analyses.

THE PLACE OF EXPERIENCE, THEORY, AND COST-EFFECTIVENESS AND COST-BENEFIT ANALYSES IN CPPOA

It seems obvious that someone trying to improve a human service system
should first understand its "crucial ingredients." This, however, is where

many well-intentioned evaluators and managers make their first mistake. Many persons approaching management and research of a human service system do not bother to become acquainted with the particular problems being addressed by the system and its procedures and targeted processes. I, for example, have seen people who know very little about drug treatment begin to assess the effectiveness and costs of drug treatment programs. Others make a more sophisticated version of the same mistake when they decide in an empirical vacuum what is crucial and what is peripheral in a treatment system and then adjust budgets accordingly. This is not a peculiarity of evaluators, either.

Traditional analyses of cost-effectiveness and cost-benefit implicitly view service systems as static entities—as "black boxes" whose inputs (costs) and outputs (effectiveness, benefits) are all that can be examined in evaluation. Some of these analyses do examine the effects of different procedures on cost-effectiveness and cost-benefit in a gross way by contrasting indices of cost-effectiveness and cost-benefit for a few programs. Essentially, this sort of comparative analysis preserves the black box idea by dividing one big black box (e.g., treatment) into several smaller ones (e.g., Treatment X, Treatment Y). Multiple black boxes, each with its own index of cost-effectiveness or cost-benefit, are then compared on the index and the best one is chosen. For example, if divorce mediation Program A had a better cost-benefit index than did divorce mediation Program B, Program A would be chosen and Program B would be terminated. The information gained may be worthwhile for the particular context in which Programs A and B would have been offered, but the findings are difficult to generalize and do not help us understand why Program A was more cost-beneficial than Program B.

Traditional procedures for cost-effectiveness and cost-benefit analysis allow only fleeting and incomplete glimpses of the relationships between resources, procedures, processes, and outcomes. The first chapters of this book describe methods of collecting and analyzing data to uncover richer and possibly more useful pictures of cost → procedure, procedure → process, and process → outcome relationships. Applying these methods to a particular service system may require education about the etiologies of the human problems being addressed by the service system under study. This means more than a cursory review of the relevant political issues and clinical and research literature. Contact with the community and experience providing the services being evaluated may be necessary to provide the foundation for a successful program analysis. What happens naturally as one works in a service system is the development of an informal understanding of why some people develop the problems dealt with by the human service system. In addition to an understanding of etiology, the practitioner perceives some psychosocial processes that could heal the problem and selects treatment procedures that should evoke those processes. In essence, the practitioner has constructed an intuitive and experientially validated model of the service system, particularly as it could be applied to a specific client. This individual-level model may be guided by a more formal system-level model that may be espoused by the director and service system charter. Individual-level and system-level models can be developed or refined for a wide variety of human services using several methods for quantifying cost → outcome relationships and also showing the potential benefits of capturing the entire cost → procedure → process → outcome relationship. These methods are the focus of the last chapter in this book.

Different theoretical approaches to the same problem may lead one to vastly different solutions. For example, considering drug abuse to be the result of reversible processes involving psychological and chemical addiction directs one toward counseling of individual drug abusers as the primary service procedure (Onken & Blaine, 1990). If, however, drug abuse is seen to be caused by a dearth of economic opportunities, the focus of human service procedures may be elimination of political and economic processes that may be responsible for economic and other oppression of minority groups. It is possible, of course, for several models of the problem to be correct and to pursue concurrent courses of action suggested by each model.

SMPs develop their models by using insights gained from practical experience and from the theoretical and research literature to guide their systematic study of service system procedures, resulting processes, outcomes, and the resources consumed by the service system. Construction of this model is the focus of cost-effectiveness analysis and of cost-benefit analysis. In both cost-effectiveness and cost-benefit analyses, resources and outcomes of a service system are measured. As detailed in coming chapters, cost-effectiveness analysis and cost-benefit analysis compare the value of resources consumed by a service system to the outcomes produced by the system.

2

Cost Assessment: Measuring the Value of Resources Used

The cost or *value* of resources that make possible health and human services can be a function of several determinants: (a) valuation strategies, (b) interest group perspectives, (c) levels of specificity, (d) flexibility of resources, (e) time and duration of assessment, and (f) focus of resources. Of course, other major determinants are the actual types and values of the resources used. This chapter examines how these determinants combine to offer alternatives for measuring the value of resources consumed in a service system.

As methods of cost assessment are described, you may experience increasing concern about the cost of collecting cost data. Fortunately, the expense of the cost assessment methods described covers a considerable range. It also may be helpful to note that resource expenditures can be measured for the period of the evaluation, or expenditures can be sampled just as outcomes are when the number of clients served exceeds the data collection capabilities of the evaluator. Because many evaluation budgets do not reflect the complete expense of collecting data on costs as well as procedures, processes, and outcomes, sampling of cost data may be necessary in lieu of comprehensive cost data, as discussed later in this chapter.

CLASSIC COST AND COST-OUTCOME ANALYSES

Cost-Effectiveness Analysis

In traditional cost-effectiveness analysis, outcomes are measured in whatever units are most appropriate: reduction in depression for programs that focus on depression and reduction in drug use for substance abuse programs. The results are ratios of cost to effectiveness (e.g., "$439 for movement of the average patient from a score in the clinically depressed range to a subclinical score on the Beck Depression Inventory" or "$24.95 per pound lost and kept off during the 10-week program.") If a program has multiple outcomes, measures of each outcome can be combined in weighted averages or other composite indices. The composite outcome measure then can be contrasted to costs. Cost and effectiveness also can be arrayed in tables or graphs so that information on cost and effectiveness is not lost in the formation of a ratio. Methods for tabular, graphic, and other ways of analyzing relationships between costs and outcomes are described in the last chapter of this book. Most cost-effectiveness analyses contrast cost and effectiveness information for one program against similar information for alternative programs to arrive at decisions about which program is most cost-effective. Similar analyses can be performed at a more specific level for alternative procedures within a single human service system.

Cost-Benefit Analysis

In traditional cost-benefit analysis, as in classic cost-effectiveness analysis, outcomes are contrasted to costs. In cost-benefit analysis, however, outcomes and costs are measured in the same units. Usually, a monetary unit, such as dollars or pounds, is used for both resources consumed and outcomes produced. By using a common measure for outcomes, diverse programs can be compared so long as analysts agree that the measures of outcome adequately capture the important program outcomes according to interest groups.

By using the same units for costs and outcomes, a ratio of outcomes to costs also can be calculated. The result of dividing dollars produced by dollars consumed is a unitless ratio—the classic *benefit-cost ratio*. Although single ratios impart some information (e.g., a ratio greater than 1:1 indicates that the program generates more value than it consumes), ratios of benefits to costs can be compared for different programs or different procedures within a program. The tabular, graphic, and other analyses that can be performed on cost and effectiveness information also can be performed on cost and benefit information. In this way, cost-benefit analysis is similar to cost-effectiveness analysis.

Although both cost-effectiveness analysis and cost-benefit analysis have long histories of use and development in economics and business (Kendall, 1971), they also can be conceptualized as subsets of cost → procedure → process → outcome analysis (CPPOA). By themselves, neither cost-effectiveness analysis nor cost-benefit analysis attempts to describe or improve on the potentially elaborate network of relationships between use of specific resources, therapeutic procedures, psychological and social processes, and achievement of interim and long-term outcomes. After costs, effectiveness, and benefits are measured, they need to be related to specific procedures and processes. This is the next step of CPPOA. Moreover, the optimum path needs to be found so that as few resources as possible are used to put into motion only those procedures that are crucial to touching off the processes that lead to the desired outcomes.

Finding this path is difficult: Many alternatives need to be considered and several tried on a pilot basis before real improvement results. Sometimes, detailed models can be manipulated to see what modifications of resources and procedures will make the biggest improvement in outcomes. Often, after the first failure or two, the model on which the earlier possible solutions were based requires revision. This "try, reflect and reanalyze, and try again" cycle is central to problem solving. Its iterations are familiar to anyone who has engaged in the day-to-day struggle of making things work when many people are involved. Its fruits are the sort of advancement that makes human services administration so intensive and, sometimes, so deeply rewarding. Its methods were reviewed earlier in a cursory way; now we turn to the specifics. This chapter focuses on the first major task in any cost-effectiveness or cost-benefit analysis: the measurement of cost.

Cost

   Cost has several very different meanings in the evaluation literature and, it can be argued, should have several more. A traditional definition of cost as it is used in economics is the amount that a consumer is willing to pay for a good or service. In human services, however, clients rarely are able to pay anything. In addition, information about alternative service sites rarely is available to consumers in the completeness required for intelligent decisions about which service to select. Furthermore, clients of some human services may not be sufficiently rational to perceive supply-demand relationships and make the rational choices that underlie the "willingness to pay" definition of cost (Katona, 1975).

   Management science approaches cost assessment by seeking to understand how costs are related to outcomes (e.g., profits) through manufacturing or service procedure (Anderson, Sweeney, & Williams, 1976). Measuring costs so they can be related to procedures and outcomes has been termed *cost analysis* and has a relatively long history (Longman, 1941/1978; Pirrong, 1993; Young, 1988). To understand, analyze, and improve linkages between resources, procedures, processes, and outcomes of service systems, cost is defined as the value of each resource that is consumed when the program implements a service procedure. Cost is not a single entity;

the sum of the many resources makes health and human services possible. The cost of any one resource also exists as different values depending on the way in which the cost is measured (Pires, 1990). Although costs often are reported in single units, such as dollars, the value of different resources may be measured most accurately in the units in which they naturally occur. For example, a person's time may be best measured in hours, whereas facilities may be best measured in square meters.

To sum up costs in a single number discards potentially important information about the diversity of resources that are used in a service system and the quantities of each resource that may be needed. Few managers or researchers would restrict themselves to measuring the outcomes of a treatment or social program with only one instrument and reporting a single result. Why should the resources that made the outcomes possible be any more restricted?

Cost can be defined in other ways. When expenditures required for certain clients in one program are increased or decreased *as a result* of another program—and when the program that caused the expenditure increase is the one being analyzed—the altered expenditures actually constitute an outcome of the program being analyzed. Suppose, for instance, that an education campaign about sexually transmitted diseases (STDs) increases visits to health clinics by persons seeking diagnoses and treatment for STDs (e.g., Diamond & Schnee, 1991). The education campaign could be said to have the outcomes of (a) increasing requests for diagnosis and treatment of STDs and (b) increasing health care costs. The STD education campaign has, as *its* costs, the value of resources consumed in implementing STD campaign procedures, such as time spent in the community talking to clients, radio spots, brochure distribution, and time spent contacting schools, religious organizations, and community representatives.

It also is possible, naturally, for a program to have as an outcome the reduction in resources expended by another program. For example, an STD education campaign should reduce health care costs in the long run by thwarting the spread of STDs and associated medical problems, sick leave, and poorer individual functioning. Whether the final outcome of the STD campaign is a net increase or decrease in health care costs depends on whether a short-term or long-term perspective is adopted and on how complete a set of outcome variables is used.

Last, costs can be measured as either (a) what actually was spent or as (b) what it usually would take to execute the procedures of the service system. The "what it would take" position on cost assessment often is used when cost data were not collected along with effectiveness data and when concerns about cost-effectiveness and cost-benefit were considered fairly late in the evaluation. It also can be argued that actual expenses may include excessive spending and that only what should have been spent should be allowed to enter the cost total. What, however, might be the result of these positions? If an evaluator is allowed to estimate costs, shouldn't the assessment of outcomes be allowed to proceed in a similar fashion? Would it be appropriate to allow outcomes to be estimated rather than measured? Should only those outcomes that should have occurred be included in a program evaluation? If outcomes deserve more attention than this, perhaps costs do as well.

In an effort to include only the important costs in resource assessment, it also might be proposed that the cost of administering a service system be excluded from cost assessment. Although this position could generate cost data specific to a procedure being studied, it neglects what often is the majority of the total program cost: the overhead. The relative size of the overhead components of health and human services need not be embarrassing, but it does need to be appreciated, measured, reported, and included in analyses that attempt to optimize cost-effectiveness and cost-benefit.

QUALITATIVE AND QUANTITATIVE DESCRIPTIONS OF RESOURCES CONSUMED IN SERVICE PROVISION

I have found it useful to remind myself that the resources consumed by a service system may be—and probably should be—as challenging to evaluate as the outcomes produced by the service system. Just as only a few of the frequent outcomes of social services are found in records maintained by most service systems, so do most program archives list only a subset of the resources consumed in treatment. Resources that require expenditures of money to be obtained typically are monitored so these data can be reported to funders and government tax collection agencies. Resources that do not involve overt transfers of funds, however, often go unreported. These resources include volunteered time and donated facilities that may be crucial ingredients in the mixture of resources that makes service procedures possible and, therefore, need to be assessed.

To really understand resource → procedure → process → outcome relationships, we need to know the types and amounts of resources consumed by the service system to implement each service procedure (Newman & Sorensen, 1985; Pires, 1990; Sorensen & Hanbery, 1979; Sorensen & Phipps, 1975). A qualitative description of resources consumed in the provision of human services begins with a list of resources used. Broadly conceived, the resources used in the provision of human services are people's time and skills, space, instruments and other equipment, supplies, finances (e.g., lines of credit), transportation, communications and information services, and sundry other resources. The quantitative portion of assessment first assigns values to these various resources and then determines how much of each type was used in providing each specific procedure to each client. For instance, resource assessment for treatment of clients with a post-traumatic stress disorder (PTSD) would include separate measurements of the amounts and values of counselor time, clinic space, biofeedback equipment use, and therapeutic drugs used. This assessment is conducted for each client separately, given that some clients consume significantly more program resources than do others (e.g., Halfon, 1990). Resources that could not be assigned to a particular procedure or client, such as bank fees paid by the clinic to maintain accounts and credit lines, are distributed over all procedures and clients. Similarly, to the expense of each treatment procedure performed on each PTSD client would be added a small portion of the salaries paid to the program administrator, office staff, and building maintenance workers. In addition, the value of clients' time spent at the clinic and going to and from it would be included in a comprehensive resource assessment, along with other client expenses, such as transportation.

TEMPORAL RESOURCES

Valuing Service Procedures Implemented by Primary Change Agents

All human services take someone's time. Temporal resources used in human services include the time and skills of therapists, clients, managers, and many other change agents. At a minimum, the clients themselves spend time in attempts at self-management or in self-help groups following referral. The amount of time devoted to applying different service procedures to a client also may differ as a function of the change agent, client, procedure, and the degree to which a procedure is to be implemented. Some fraction of the time of administrative staff also contributes, most likely, to treatment (e.g., running the payroll that keeps therapists working at the clinic). For these reasons, the amount of time spent by each change agent on each procedure for each client needs to be measured separately for each episode of service.

Valuing Time Spent in Treatment Procedures

A microlevel strategy for valuing the different types and amounts of temporal resources devoted to different clients and procedures is relatively simple, if laborious: Measure the time spent by each agent with each client performing each procedure. These durations then are multiplied by the value of the agent's activities per unit time, calculated by one of the procedures to be discussed, to arrive at the value of the agent's time for a particular procedure for a particular client.

The value of different agents' time can be assessed according to their education, their practical training, years of experience in similar positions, their demonstrated effectiveness in solving human problems—or their salaries. The *operations valuation* strategy would be to use the actual money paid to operate the program: salaries. The *replacement value* of the change agent's time would be what it would cost to hire someone to do the same job, at a similar level of competency, as the current change agent. Extremely dedicated agents can be costly to replace, but generally, replacement value of personnel would be salary and benefits plus initial training costs (to bring a new agent up to speed). The *opportunity value* strategy would measure the value of a change agent's time according to the next best possible use of that time. Supposing that the change agent would seek a similar position if they could not participate in the service system under study, the opportunity value of their time would be the standard pay scales or grade levels established by federal and state governments for health and human services for personnel with similar education, experience, and performance evaluations. Using pay scales rather than salaries can yield more generalizable comparisons between service systems in regions that have different standards of living and thus offer different salaries for the same work. Common units are *dollars per hour,* although therapist hours and administrative staff hours are alternative units: Money actually need not be involved. If pay scales list only annual salaries, hourly rates of pay can be calculated by dividing the salary by the number of hours worked in a usual year (e.g., [$60,000/year] ÷ [50 working weeks/year × 40 hours/week] = $60,000/year ÷ 2,000 hours/year = $30/hour). To be accurate and comprehensive, salary figures should include not only gross income but also the estimated monetary value of health care, life insurance, pension contributions, medical leaves, vacation pay, and other benefits paid for by the employer plus perquisites such as use of a vehicle for personal business and free or subsidized room and board.

The rate of pay calculated from salary and benefits paid to change agents may not accurately reflect the replacement or opportunity value of their program activities in at least two respects. First, the rate of pay received by a person may not match their actual expertise or even their education and experience. This is most often found in persons who are underemployed. They may have taken the position because of its less tangible benefits, such as flexibility of working hours or the opportunity to receive training in the provision of human services. In human services especially, underemployment may result from the desire of previously helped clients to help others who need services similar to those they once received. An extreme case of underemployment is that of clinical psychology or social work graduate students whose time may be quite valuable but who are paid nothing for their internship.

It is especially likely that the total salary plus benefits paid during a time period will not always represent the total value of time spent by an agent in service activities. Even if the actual rate of pay exactly matches the rate prescribed by education and experience or whatever criteria have been adopted, the salary and benefits paid may be the same from month to month even though the time spent in service activities varies considerably between months. Some investigators have found that the total value of time spent by some persons in treatment activities during some time periods can be substantially less than would be expected on the basis of their monthly salary (Yates, Haven, & Thoresen, 1979). Fluctuations in demand during another time period, of course, might cause the same persons to spend considerably more time in service activities during that period than was justified by their monthly salary.

Collecting Temporal Resource Data: Paper and Computer Methods

The next task in this detailed or microlevel assessment of the value of personnel time is to measure the amount of time spent by change agents in service-related activities. To collect data to later be able to assess the value of resources devoted to each procedure for each client, these time data need to be measured separately for each application of each procedure by each agent to each client. This assessment method also generates some variance in cost data, which reflects real differences in the resources devoted to servicing different clients (Beecham, Knapp, & Fenyo, 1991). Variance in cost values also is useful for later statistical analyses of the contributions of different resources to various procedures, processes, and outcomes. Time spent performing different service procedures (e.g., a counseling session, a medical examination, a skills-training session) can be recorded in many ways.

There are several options for determining the amount of time spent by each change agent performing each treatment procedure. Yates et al. (1979)

Table 2.1

Basic Form for Self-Report of Service-Related Activities

Service-Related Activities	Time Period 1	Time Period 2	. . .	Time Period n	Totals
Direct services					
Activity 1					
Activity 2					
. . .					
Activity a					
Totals					

asked all staff and volunteers at a residential program for predelinquent youth to record all time spent in program-related activities on a weekly form of the sort shown in Table 2.1. The form developed by Yates et al. included 16 columns (for activities in the morning and evening of each day, plus totals for morning and evening) and 12 rows (for specific types of activities ranging from "with Learning House children" and "with Learning House parents" to "preparing for counseling," "reading," and "other"). Using these forms, data on staff time were collected for a random sample of weeks in the study period. Staff seemed motivated to complete the forms because the results showed the great amount of time they spent in treatment-related activities. This recording format did not, however, allow separation of the amount of time devoted to specific clients. Yates et al. were forced to assume that staff members spent equal amounts of time with each client, which probably was not the case.

Often, the most practical method of recording accurate data is for each agent to keep track of the amount of time they spend with each client doing each treatment procedure. When numerous service activities are of short duration and are performed on many clients in a manner that cannot be readily predicted from schedules, more accurate cost data may be obtained by asking change agents to record service type, duration, and target immediately following delivery of the service. A sample form for doing this is shown in Table 2.2. In this spreadsheet-style log, clients are listed in columns and treatment procedures are listed in rows. Time spent administering a procedure to a client is recorded in the cell at the intersection of the client's column and the procedure's row. If the agent works with more clients than can be listed across the top of one sheet, more sheets can be added. A separate set of sheets can be used each day. Most forms of CPPOA are much easier if cost data are available in a computer format. Entering

Table 2.2

Spreadsheet for Recording Change Agent Activity

	Client				
Service Procedures	*012*	*034*	*035*	*043*	*051*
Intake and orientation					
Individual counseling					
Dealing with affect					
Cognitive skill instruction					
Addressing basic needs					
Legal services and referrals					
Medical condition and					
complications					
Engagement and interaction					
Self-management training					
Behavioral contracting					
Educational group					
Medical diagnosis					
Relapse-prevention training					
Case review and conference					
Recording, collecting data					

data by hand into a computer from paper spreadsheets such as Table 2.2 requires time and skill. Optical character recognition devices can speed entry of data from paper spreadsheets into computer formats and now are available as part of inexpensive fax software (e.g., Delrina Technology, 1992).

Management of all these cost data can be facilitated by collecting data on computer spreadsheets instead of paper spreadsheets and by linking to a central database the spreadsheets that appear on each change agent's computer display. Agents can enter time values onto the computer screen or on a tablet, and the centralized database can compile information for procedures and clients over time. If agents are not comfortable with computers or if computers are not available for individual agents, mark-sense forms (with ovals that are filled in with a No. 2 pencil) can be designed to allow recording of time spent by each agent on each procedure for each client. A disadvantage of this approach over the columns-and-rows method shown in Table 2.2 is that a separate form needs to be completed each time an agent implements one or more procedures with a client. An advantage of the mark-sense forms is that the sheets can be run through a mark-sense reader for rapid, low-cost entry into computer databases.

For example, Yates, Besteman, Filipczak, and Greenfield (1993) obtained data on the amount of time spent by substance abuse counselors in individual counseling sessions by asking them to complete a mark-sense form after each session. The form was designed to be filled out with a minimum of time and effort and to be read directly into the cost database by an automated mark-sense form reader connected to a personal computer. Sections of the form provided entry formats for dates of sessions, counselor and client identification numbers, clinic name, minutes of session time, 27 types of service procedures, 9 types of referral, and 14 approaches to treatment (e.g., behavioral, reality therapy). Similar computer mark-sense forms were developed for group therapy sessions, child-sitting at the clinic, medical services rendered, and medical referrals provided. Daily feedback to staff and the clinic director on the number of mark-sense forms submitted, versus the approximate number expected based on appointment and attendance records kept by the clinic receptionist, helped staff complete and submit forms before leaving the service system for the day.

Even mark-sense forms may, however, be too much of a hassle for some busy professionals. Self-reporting time spent in specific activities with each client also may be reactive; reporting time spent in specific activities may change how service agents allocate their time among those activities. Alternative methods of recording time spent conducting treatment-related procedures include using commercially available wands, cards, or other forms of portable bar code readers to record activities in a manner similar to procedures used in libraries to record books and tapes borrowed and used in stores to record merchandise purchased. By passing the wand or card over different bar codes, the agent could record resource use sentences (e.g., [change agent] performed for [client] [Procedure 1] for [Duration 1], [Procedure 2] for [Duration 2], . . . and [Procedure P] for [Duration P] on [date] at [site].) These sorts of sentences were used by Yates (1975; see also Yates, 1980a) in the initial development of an observation system for client behavior. Many of these data sentences can be stored in electronic wands or "smart cards" powered by small batteries. At the end of the day, the bar code readers-storage devices can be turned in for downloading to computer files. The output of the readers often is either a record of keystrokes or simple numbers and letters that can be used for data input without additional programming. Systems using bar code wands and computer software and hardware have been developed for monitoring progress of severely retarded adults in treatment plans. Translation of these methods to cost assessment should be straightforward.

To further reduce demands on staff and clients for active participation in the collection of cost data, a passive system for recording resource data also could be developed. A combination of identity badges or pins worn by staff and clients and electronic badge or pin monitors placed in rooms could provide central computers with minute-by-minute information on the how much time staff and clients spent in the same room. Staff would have to add information on the particular procedures performed, however. The hardware for this data collection methodology is available; similar systems are common in industrial research and development settings where security or employee monitoring is important.

Putting Value and Time Data Together

To arrive at a number expressing the total value of resources expended by a particular change agent in services, the amount of time spent by that agent is multiplied by the value of that agent's activity per unit time. For example, a part-time counselor who devotes 10 hours to direct service and whose value is set at $30 per hour according to education and experience can be said to have expended 10 hours × $30/hour = $300 of activity resources. To be used in CPPOA later, these costs need to be available for each client separately and for each major treatment procedure performed by each change agent on that client. For instance, a psychologist, social worker, nurse, and child care worker all might be providing direct services to families at risk. The clinician might spend 25 minutes helping the mother learn to cope with her anger about the affair that contributed to the divorce. The remaining 25 minutes might be spent training the mother in cognitive problem-solving skills. The social worker then could work with the mother to apply the problem-solving skill to the pressing issues of finding inexpensive housing, a part-time job, and child care. This might require 40 minutes. Arranging for referrals to legal counsel to improve the chances of receiving child support could take another 10 minutes. A nurse might then see the mother for 20 minutes to review the results of her pregnancy test and to discuss alternatives for dealing with an STD also found during examination. Another 10 minutes of unscheduled time might then be spent with the psychologist, learning to deal with the renewed anger and again applying problem-solving steps for concrete coping strategies. During this 2-hour period, a child care worker would have supervised the play of the young children in the family. At a case conference the next morning, all four professionals might meet to discuss new and continuing clients, including 10 minutes spent discussing this family. Table 2.3 illustrates the distribution of time by these agents among these activities. Table 2.4 demonstrates how the different pay rates shown under each agent label and service procedure could be used to calculate different values for the procedures.

Table 2.3

Valuing Activities of Change Agents in a Service System for Families at Risk

	Change Agents			
	Psychologist	Social Worker	Nurse	Child Care Worker
Dealing with affect	25 minutes			
Cognitive skill instruction	25 minutes			
Addressing basic needs		40 minutes		
Legal services and referrals		10 minutes		
Medical condition and complications			20 minutes	
Engagement and interaction				120 minutes
Case review and conference	10 minutes	10 minutes	10 minutes	10 minutes
Total	60	60	30	130

Table 2.4

Valuing Activities of Change Agents in a Service System for Families at Risk: Monetizing Time Spent by Each Agent in Each Activity for One Family

	Change Agents			
	Psychologist ($40/hour)	Social Worker ($30/hour)	Nurse ($25/hour)	Child Care Worker ($10/hour)
Dealing with affect	$16.67			
Cognitive skill instruction	$16.67			
Addressing basic needs		$20.00		
Legal services and referrals		$5.00		
Medical condition and complications			$8.33	
Engagement and interaction				$20.00
Case review and conference	$8.33	$5.00	$4.17	$1.67
Total	$41.67	$30.00	$12.50	$21.67

Estimating Costs per Procedure
per Client Without All the Data

If time data are not recorded separately for each procedure administered to each client each day, there are several options for estimating the cost per procedure for a client. If a standard set of procedures is performed reliably at treatment sessions, the time spent with the client can be divided by the number of procedures delivered to arrive at the time spent per procedure. If some of the procedures performed are known to require more time than others, the total time can be allocated in proportion to the relative amount of time that each procedure should take. For example, if 50 minutes are spent with an abused spouse to provide simple assessment, some brief counseling, and several referrals, it might be estimated that the written referrals required about half the time of the assessment, which itself took about the same time as the counseling. If so, the value of that 50-minute session would be distributed as 1 part referrals, 2 parts assessment, and 2 parts counseling, or 10, 20, and 20 minutes for referral, assessment, and counseling respectively. If some activities are conducted simultaneously, such as some forms of counseling and diagnosis, the total time spent in the joint activities can be allocated equally between those activities. For instance, 10 minutes of combined counseling and diagnosis could be considered as 5 minutes for counseling and 5 minutes for diagnosis. If the activity really is a joint activity in which each component supports the other, however, perhaps it should receive its own procedure category.

It would, of course, be better to record the actual amount of time spent delivering each procedure to the client. It is possible, however, that other studies have measured the amount of time required to perform each of the procedures involved in the agent-client contact. In that case, the standard times per procedure can be used so long as their sum does not exceed the total duration recorded for the service (in which case a proportional reduction would have to be performed in the time allowed for each procedure). Finally, the value of the agent's time then can be combined with data on the amount of the agent's time to estimate the cost per procedure per client.

What to Do With Overhead Time
From Change Agents

It is likely that some time spent by change agents with clients is not devoted to any specific procedure but instead is spent getting to know the client or in opening and closing pleasantries. These usually are important activities and, in any case, are real resources being spent. This sort of overhead time needs to be allocated evenly among all procedures performed for all clients during the session as a sort of overhead expense. In the same manner, time spent by administrators and office staff certainly cannot be excluded from cost assessment; these, too, are valuable resources that contribute indirectly to treatment and add to its cost.

Valuing Clients' Time

Primary Clients

The time spent by change agents, such as therapists, in executing human service procedures usually is the most valuable and important resource to be measured in cost-effectiveness analysis, cost-benefit analysis, and full CPPOA. The time devoted by clients to the implementation of human services is similarly crucial, even though it often is viewed as having no monetary or other value. From the interest group perspectives of primary and secondary clients, it can be argued strongly that client time is important and should be assessed and valued. Without the time of clients, after all, no human service can be provided.

Change agent and researcher perspectives on cost assessment also may favor assessment of temporal resources provided by clients to services. Clients who do not appear for appointments, who disappear when change agents attempt to contact them in the community, and who do not follow advice to do certain things at home and seek certain other services, will likely be unsuccessful. Knowing the amount of time spent by each client doing different things recommended by change agents, and other measures of client participation in service provision, may provide insights into and predictors of attrition from therapy and in other services (Yates, 1978). Thus, the scientist perspective also may support collection of data on the amount of clients' temporal resources that are consumed.

The amount of time spent by clients receiving services and in activities suggested by service agents can be assessed by spreadsheet logs similar to those completed by primary change agents. Instead of listing different clients in different columns, however, each column can be for a different day. Sufficient room may be available for the client to record participation in each treatment procedure for each day of an entire month. Clients typically need guidance in making entries on the form for the first few days and may need the purpose of the forms explained. Some clients need assistance due to poor reading skills or low motivation for form completion. Soon, however, primary clients may become more invested in procedures of treatment as a result of using these forms. Essentially, the forms provide a menu of service procedures from which the primary change agent and the client can choose to change the client's psychology, social circumstances, and even aspects of the client's biology (e.g., chemical addiction). Thus, measurement of the time invested by clients in program activities has the potential to be somewhat empowering to clients. The selective recording and omission of activities by clients also may enlighten change agents and scientists as to the service procedures that clients do and do not perceive as having occurred.

An alternative to asking clients to complete forms is, of course, to interview them verbally. Self-reports of services used and received have proven reliable and valid. Ratings of service use derived from videotapes of client interviews and reports of services used by homeless mentally ill clients were found by Calsyn, Allen, Morse, Smith, and Tempelhoff (1993) to be quite reliable, with the exception of some mental health and health services. Direct reports from clients of services used also agreed significantly with reports of key informants in local service organizations, with the exception of therapy and some health-related services. The services queried by Calsyn et al. (1993) were transitional and long-term housing, employment, job training, entitlements, welfare benefits, clothing, medical care, dental care, psychiatric emergency room visits, psychotropic medication, psychotherapy, counseling, mental health and other day programs, other mental health services, and legal and supportive services.

The value of time spent by primary clients in service-related activities too often is treated as nil. Although it can be useful to simply know the number of hours required of clients by a service program, the opportunity cost of that time often is substantial. Even if it is time well spent, according to cost-benefit analysis, it is time that could have been spent in other activities. Clients employed or working in the home can have concrete, monetary values assigned to their time if time spent in service activities could have been spent making money or taking care of the household, children, or others (e.g., an elderly parent). These temporal opportunity costs can be calculated by multiplying the pay rate for the employed client or for personnel who provide similar services for pay, by the time spent in treatment.

For example, a 1-hour session with a psychiatric social worker during the weekday might be valued from the primary client perspective as opportunity-costing him or her $35 for time spent in the session that could have been spent earning income. The client also could view as an opportunity cost the half-hour spent going to and from the session (as $20, possibly), plus $5 for transportation expenses. To this $60 "bill" then could be added the fee charged for the session, to arrive at the total cost of the session from the perspective of the primary client. The cost of a session held before or after work should exclude a monetary value for primary client time. This exclusion seems justified if the client would not have spent that time in other potentially income-enhancing activities and if the client would not have spent the time at home either caring for children or performing home or vehicle maintenance.

To arrive at an accurate value for the time of clients when adopting the perspective of primary or secondary clients, the specifics of each case need to be considered. For instance, if unemployed clients would have spent session time caring for their young children, their mates might have been able to spend that time in part-time jobs or working in income-producing forms of self-employment. In this case, the value of the client's time could be quantified as the value of the spouse's employment that was foregone by the client attending a session. Again, however, the particulars of the case dictate the exact manner of cost assessment. If the children could have been watched by a child sitter or professional child care provider while the mate worked, then the money that had to be paid to that child sitter or care provider better reflects the opportunity cost of time spent by the client in treatment.

Secondary Clients

When significant others in the client's environment are involved in treatment activities, the temporal resources they expend in those activities also can be included in cost assessment. The value of time spent by secondary clients requires the same sort of attention to individual cases that is needed in valuation of the time spent by primary clients, as just discussed. Logs such as those completed by change agents and primary clients are appropriate if secondary clients participate in services and suggested activities regularly. An example of this would be a weekly family therapy session attended by the spouse and children of the client. "Homework," such as monitoring of arguments and pleasant activities by a mate, could be useful in assessing the cost of couples therapy. Time spent by parents administering a token economy to their child also would be a temporal resource to be recorded for secondary clients. If secondary clients participate infrequently or irregularly in service actions, questionnaires or phone contacts may be sufficient to capture the amount of time they invest in therapy. This can be an area of considerable expenditure of societal, if not monetary, resources. Franks (1987), for instance, found that the average family of a schizophrenic individual reported spending $7,980 in uncompensated time for the support, treatment, care giving, recreation, and related activities for their schizophrenic member.

Not including secondary client temporal resources in estimates of the costs of outpatient versus inpatient programs for schizophrenics could result in real misunderstanding of the value, types, and sources of resources consumed by the alternative programs. For example, McGuire (1991) found that care of schizophrenics at home required almost twice the

Table 2.5

Survey of Time Allocation

To better estimate the cost of our research, clinical, and other activities, we need some
information on how you allocate your time during the specified week. In advance,
thank you for your time in completing this questionnaire.

For the Week of					
___/___/9__ Through		*Visits to*	*Writing,*	*Phone*	
___/___/9__	*Meetings*	*Clinics*	*Reading*	*Contacts*	*Other*
Clinical activities					
Clinic 1					
Clinic 2					
Hospital					
Other direct service					
Clinic administration					
Research activities					
Clinic 1					
Clinic 2					
Hospital					
Other research					
Proposal development					
Clinic administration					

resources as care in a public facility. The $cost_{home}/cost_{public\ facility}$ ratio was
$15,160/$7,647 or 1.98, including both monetary outlays and the value of
time devoted by the family to treatment-related activities. This cost-cost
ratio was essentially the same when viewed from the operations perspective
of purely money units: $4,422/$2,059 = 2.15.

Assessing and Allocating Overhead Temporal Resources

The value of overhead staff's time can be obtained from the usual pay rates
based on education and experience. The time they provide can be assessed
with logs similar to those described earlier. Table 2.5, similar to a form
developed by Yates et al. (1993), provides an example of this sort of log. To
facilitate other studies, it might be useful to record separately the amount of
time spent in staff meetings versus community relations and fund raising. If a
manager spends a specific amount of time focusing on a single client (e.g., in
a case conference), that could be recorded and later allocated directly to the
cost figure for that client. This client-specific temporal resource allocation
still cannot be assigned to a particular treatment procedure, however.

As when estimating the cost per procedure per client when one has only concrete data on the cost per client, temporal overhead costs can be distributed over all clients (and all procedures performed for each client) equally. An alternative and possibly more accurate strategy is to allocate more of the resources to clients who consume more direct service time and to allocate more of that resource within clients to allocate more of that resource to procedures that take more direct service time. The latter approach to distributing the expense of temporal resources that contribute indirectly to treatment procedures will generate more accurate cost estimates if there is considerable disparity in the amount of time spent by persons working directly with different clients. This assessment method also avoids excessive overhead charges to clients who attend only a few sessions.

For example, if 50 clients were seen during a given day and the clinic director's salary of $500 for that day had to be distributed equally over each client, $10 of the director's time would be added to the cost of treating each client. If 20 clients had been seen for only 10 minutes each and 30 others for 60 minutes each, however, it would make more sense to add a smaller amount of overhead charge to the cost of treating clients who used only 10 minutes of direct service resources and to add a larger charge to the cost of treating clients who used 60 minutes of direct service resources. In this case, the key to finding the exact smaller or larger amount to add is to figure the basic dollars of overhead salary per minute. This is arrived at by dividing the total for overhead for the time period (e.g., the $500 of director salary for the day) by total minutes of client services delivered. That's $500 ÷ [(20 clients × 10 minutes) + (30 clients × 60 minutes)] = $500 ÷ [200 + 1800] = $500 ÷ 2000 client-minutes = $0.25/client-minute. Each 10-minute client is, then, charged 10 minutes × $0.25/client-minute = $2.50 and each 60-minute client is charged 60 minutes × $0.25/client-minute = $15.00, of the temporal resources devoted by the clinic director.

The same basic procedure also can be used to distribute indirectly applied temporal resources across clients who each use a service for a different amount of time. Similar calculations can be used to distribute nonpersonnel overhead resources, such as space in an office building, office equipment, or insurance, over clients.

SPATIAL RESOURCES: FACILITIES

The actual sites at which health and human services are provided can vary greatly between services: Clinics, hospitals, homes, mobile homes, shelters, trailers, or sidewalks or streets can be used. Human services can seem siteless, as when they are provided via phone or video or computer link, or through use of a manual. Physical sites are involved in apparently siteless services as well (e.g., the home office area from which a telephone counselor might operate). The sites of service delivery and of administrative services are spatial resources that often represent the second largest monetary cost (after personnel).

Issues of Depreciation Periods and Depreciation Rates

The overall value of space used in the provision or management of human services can be established according to the rental or lease rate for the office or building used. If the space is donated or is in a building built and operated by government agencies, its opportunity cost or replacement value usually can be estimated by taking the average of local square-foot rates for rent or lease of similar space in a similar neighborhood during the same period of time. Alternatively, the loss of value or depreciation experienced by the building during the period of use can be considered the cost of its use. McGuire (1991) suggests adding to the depreciation the opportunity cost of investing funds in the building as opposed to the next best investment.

Renovations commonly performed when a service system begins to use a facility also should be included. If not reflected in the rental or lease rate, the cost of renovations can be distributed over a standard period of depreciation and added to annual figures for rent or lease. Standard accounting practices common in computation of income tax deductions often use a 30-year figure for residential housing (as most people who have used home office deductions for consulting or private practice probably know), but longer periods apply to office space in many buildings. Published accounting guidelines can be consulted to determine the most appropriate period for depreciation. The exact assumptions made for depreciation and inflation rates can alter substantially the conclusions about the relative costs of alternative programs (McGuire, 1991).

The choice of the period over which the space loses its value (the depreciation period) can affect spatial costs substantially. Choosing a 40-year rather than a 20-year period could halve annual spatial resource costs as the same expense (e.g., $800,000 purchase price for an office building) would be spread out over twice the period (e.g., $40,000 for each of 20 years versus $20,000 for each of 40 years). Because depreciation often is not constant, however, the depreciation period and the time during that period at which cost assessment is conducted may affect costs, too. If the loss of value of a resource is accelerated (i.e., occurring primarily in the early years of use, as when purchasing a new car or computer), cost estimates based on depreciation will be higher per client in the earlier years of the period. If the loss of value of a resource is skewed toward the later years (as is the case with many buildings), however, costs based on depreciation should be higher in the later years.

These effects of time of assessment on cost can be viewed as problems to be adjusted for or as reflecting actual change in the value of a resource. At first glance, it seems incorrect and even unfair to assign a higher cost to treatment of a client if the client was seen earlier in a depreciation period and a lower cost if the client was seen later in the depreciation period. Replacement value is, however, substantially lower for cars and computers just a year after purchase, whereas maintenance expenses do mount in buildings only in later years of their deprecation period (e.g., the roof needs replacing and plumbing clogs with mineral deposits). Assuming a constant rate of depreciation of a spatial or other resource assumes that maintenance expenses also will be constant, which is itself unlikely. As long as the same commonly accepted accounting practices of periods and rates of depreciation are applied to all procedures (including different treatment programs), the results are likely to be fair and accurate cost assessments.

Other Spatial Cost Issues

Whether lease, rent, or depreciation costs are used to assess the basic value of spatial resources used, related expenses, such as heating and cooling, electricity, gas, and automated security and fire safety alarm systems, also need to be considered. If cleaning and maintenance services are contracted to an external enterprise and thus are not considered in temporal resource itemizations, they need to be added to the total for spatial resources.

The total cost of a facility then can be apportioned among clients and procedures. For instance, the sum of all spatial resources for the month of May at a shelter for homeless women could be divided by the sum of the census for the shelter each night during May to figure the cost per person per night. Comparable facilities might be available at $1,000 per night, for example, and having 50, 40, and 55 women in the shelter on three consecutive nights would result in a spatial cost of $(\$1,000 \times 3) \div (50 + 40 + 55)$ = $20.69 per woman per night. At a mental health clinic, the total spatial cost for a day could be divided by the number of clients seen that day to estimate the value of spatial resources devoted to each client that day. In this way, clients who consumed more facilities resources would have more facilities costs assigned to them. If some clients spent considerably longer periods of time in a clinic during the day than did other clients, those who spent more time in the facility should bear a larger proportion of the cost of that facility that day. For example, if one former substance abuser spent 50 minutes receiving methadone maintenance during a month but another former substance abuser spent 300 minutes in counseling sessions that month, the total space cost for the month could be divided not by the number of clients seen but by the total minutes of services offered to clients (e.g., [spatial cost for the month] ÷ [50 + 300 + . . .]). To arrive at a total facilities cost for the client for that month, this spatial cost per minute then would be multiplied by the number of minutes the client was seen.

Services that use donated or public facilities may wish to exclude spatial costs from enumeration. To fully describe the resources used by the service, however, spatial resources need to be quantified for meaningful CPPOA. For a limited measurement of cost, cost-effectiveness, or cost-benefit, some service systems still may wish to exclude the monetary value of their so-called free facilities. It seems best, however, to use the replacement or opportunity value approach and to obtain an actual cost figure for the spatial resources consumed. Some may argue that being able to obtain donated facilities is a virtue that should be rewarded with lower cost figures. Indeed, it is likely that an opportunity value approach will yield a lower figure for the donated facilities because the donor could not find a lucrative alternative use for the facility. Nevertheless, to help others to understand the type and amount of spatial resources needed, it seems important to include a detailed accounting of the spatial resources used, whether or not monetary values are assigned to these resources.

Last, secondary client expenses for spatial and other nontemporal resources may be considerable for some clients. For example, Franks (1987) found that families of schizophrenics spent an average of $3,539 each year for their schizophrenic member's lodging, food, transportation, and other expenses. Not making this explicit could make less obvious the negative effects of deinstitutionalization. Assessing these and other costs to secondary clients could help families make more effective arguments for compensation.

EQUIPMENT, FURNITURE

Some service procedures require the use of equipment, and most use furniture. Biofeedback equipment may be an integral component of some chronic pain treatment, for example, and personal digital assistants may be used to facilitate monitoring, goal setting, and other procedures in self-management of food intake or exercise (Reynolds, 1987). Copiers, computers, telephone systems, fax machines, Rolodexes, desks, file cabinets, chairs, pictures, plants, carpets, and other furnishings all are resources that contribute, however indirectly, to the provision of services. The cost of this equipment on the open retail market may be a reasonably accurate measure of its total value, almost regardless of the perspective used in cost assessment. The contribution made by the apparatus to treatment of a particular client can be estimated by dividing the number of equipment use episodes that occurred during a period of time into the amount of value lost due to use over the same period. For instance, if the depreciation of a biofeedback system was $3,000 for the second year of operation and if 300 biofeedback sessions were held using the equipment during the same year, the cost per client for that year would be $3,000 ÷ 300 = $10. As with cost assessments based on depreciation of spatial resources, there are issues about the length of the depreciation period used and whether to use accelerated or straight-line depreciation schedules.

It sometimes is difficult to assign these equipment and furnishings costs to particular treatment procedures. Although furniture may have been purchased at some point in the murky past, its replacement value can be estimated by the cost of leasing similar furniture in similar condition or by the payments required for loans that would allow purchase of similar furniture. More complex calculations could be performed to estimate the depreciation value of the furniture. It is possible that not all clients should have furniture costs added to their tally. Obviously, clients who are seen exclusively in their homes or in the community should be charged for only a portion of the furniture and other resources used at the administrative headquarters of an outreach program.

SUPPLIES: MATERIAL RESOURCES

Therapeutic Drugs and Other Client-Specific Consumables

The easiest material resource to cost is the simple object that one hands the client once and that is not reusable. Whether a form, a condom, or a therapeutic drug, this discrete item can be measured for cost using the value paid for it on the open market. If it was donated, the comprehensive approach to cost assessment would suggest that the cost for purchasing an equivalent item should be used. The replacement cost of a donated item is an alternative approach that may yield a similar value.

Sundry Supplies

The paper, toner, folders, calendars, coffee, cleaning fluid, and numerous other supplies consumed in most human service systems are best valued at their cost on the open market. Usually, these resources are difficult to allocate to any specific procedures or clients and therefore need to be distributed overall just as any other overhead resource would be. Briefly, the cost of supplies can be figured for each client by dividing the total cost of supplies used during a time period by the number of client service episodes conducted during that period. Figuring this cost requires that a basic inventory system be in operation to allow reckoning of how much of the supply was consumed.

It may be simplest to begin by settling on a standard period of time—a month, for example—over which the number of client service episodes is recorded. A birth control and birth options clinic might report the number of client interviews and follow-up sessions conducted during May, for instance. A clipboard on which counselors recorded supplies removed from a storeroom might show that various amounts of paper clips, note pads, and computer disks had been removed for use during May. The total cost of these supplies could be divided by the number of client interviews and follow-up visits to figure the cost of supplies per service episode. This cost then could be added to other costs being computed for each episode.

It is possible that the value of some supplies can be assigned to specific procedures. In this case, supplies costs should be levied only on the clients who received those procedures. Clients receiving acupuncture or biofeedback procedures, for example, should have any supplies used in acupuncture or biofeedback and any office supplies used by the acupuncture or biofeedback specialist added to their cost total and to no other clients'.

PSYCHOLOGICAL RESOURCES

A resource that often is in short supply in human services, on one or both sides of the counter, desk, or interview room, is the ability to tolerate and cope with difficulties, changes in lifestyle, major life events, and daily hassles. Psychological resources are more often advocated for assessment when the perspectives of change agents or scientists are used. Primary and secondary clients also may lend their support to valuation strategies for psychological resources once the nature of the resource is explained to them. The value of psychological resources has risen in importance in the evaluation literature to the point where it is considered alongside the monetary cost of treatment for disorders such as schizophrenia (Andreasen, 1991).

Psychological resources probably are related to psychological skills for management of one's own affect, cognition, and behavior. Psychological resources also seem to have constraints, as does any other resource. That is, psychological resources seem limited in terms of how much one can handle during a particular period of time before one can handle no more (at least without resorting to desperate coping mechanisms). In addition to self-management capabilities, psychological resources that enable certain therapeutic procedures to be enacted can include social skills and even verbal and mathematical capabilities. These skills may be important to assess as determinants of service outcome because the skills of change agents and clients interact with service procedures to result in different changes in client processes, but the skills are not a resource that is expended.

Tolerance, however, can be exhausted. The stresses caused by use of a service procedure may be a psychological cost that is important not only in a personal sense to clients but also in its potential effects on clients' continuance or cessation of participation in service provision. Patients who find a treatment too difficult or personally stressful may well drop out (Williams & Yates, 1993). A treatment that keeps stresses below the maximum tolerable level may require more sessions but may keep a client in treatment long enough to benefit from it. Even if a client continues to attend most sessions and groups, he or she may find some procedures too difficult or stressful and may stop performing them, thus diminishing program effectiveness and benefits. To understand the psychological resources that may be required by different service procedures and to better comprehend and predict cessation of client participation in treatment procedures or treatment as a whole, the psychological costs of each major treatment procedure will most likely need to be assessed.

Psychological resources can be measured quickly and with some reliability and validity by simple rating scales. Different components of treatment programs have been shown to have substantially different subjective costs (Yates, 1978). To assess these psychological costs, clients can be asked to rate the stress or difficulty or hassle of each major service component on a 5-point, 7-point, or 10-point scale. Endpoints can be labeled *not at all stressful* versus *extremely stressful* or *not at all difficult* versus *extremely difficult* or *no problem* versus *an incredible hassle*. Each service component can be rated separately for psychological cost using straightforward questionnaires, as shown in Table 2.6.

Table 2.6

Assessment of Psychological Resource Constraints

Service Procedures	Low[a]									High[b]
(Service Procedure 1 described briefly, in lay terms)	1	2	3	4	5	6	7	8	9	10
(Service Procedure 2 described briefly, in lay terms)	1	2	3	4	5	6	7	8	9	10
...										
(Service Procedure j described briefly, in lay terms)	1	2	3	4	5	6	7	8	9	10

a. The time and energy required to do this part of the program, and the hassle of doing it, are extremely *low* for me.

b. The time and energy required to do this part of the program, and the hassle of doing it, are extremely *high* for me.

The ratings of procedure difficulty can have reasonable reliability and validity. For example, Williams and Yates (1993) found that, as expected, these ratings were correlated significantly and negatively with the degree to which clients said they would participate in that procedure ($rs = -.29$ and $-.39$ at earlier and later points in treatment) and significantly and negatively with self-efficacy expectancies ($rs = -.29$ and $-.40$ at earlier and later times in treatment). These estimates also may allow prediction of whether treatment will or will not be successful, based on the psychological benefits and psychological costs perceived by the client for the particular combination of components provided (Yates, 1987).

Other psychological costs exacted by some human services deserve mention even if they are challenging to quantify. Some services, such as alcohol detoxification, result not only in a high if temporary degree of discomfort but also leave the patient with a painfully heightened awareness of how he or she has harmed others. The anger at others and at oneself that often emerges during recovery from heroin or alcohol abuse is a very real cost of treatment. The debt that many former substance abusers feel they owe the community, and that they repay with community service and sponsorship of others in recovery, can be viewed as another important resource for and cost of substance use cessation services. Most of these psychological costs really are outcomes of treatment, however, rather than costs and should be treated as such. Participation in many human services often results, unfortunately, in negative stigma for clients. Receiving income maintenance payments, food stamps, drug abuse treatment, or psychotherapy may decrease the esteem with which one is regarded by others—and by oneself. Stigmatization costs can be very real, but they also are outcomes of services rather than resources used to perform treatment procedures.

OTHER RESOURCES

Human service systems are so diverse that each may consume types of resources that have not been anticipated here. It is very likely, however, that these new types of resources can be assessed using one or more of the methods described. There is one additional class of resources that deserves special mention: access to the resources of other services.

External Services Such as
Communications and Information Services

Increasingly, human services use modern communications and computing services to extend their reach while controlling costs. Access to comprehensive computer reference databases allows remote services to stay informed about new therapeutic techniques and new funding opportunities, for example, to better compete with more centrally located services for funds and clients. Combinations of computer and video linkages allow facilities to be distributed across many neighborhoods and communities and yet be managed centrally. Communications services, including telephone services, high-speed modems, video cable, optical fiber access, and general network services (e.g., Internet) used by some human service facilities are additional costs. Information services also include charges for searching private and public databases for information about theory, diagnosis, and treatment of human problems on access gateways such as CompuServe©. These services typically are charged monthly based on usage, with fixed minima for basic services, and can be distributed over clients like any other overhead resource. If services are provided to a particular client primarily via computer or telephone linkage, of course, a portion of the service should be allocated directly to cost of treatment for the client.

Financing: Access to Monetary Resources

Access to a line of credit is essential for any human service that begins operation with few capital reserves and receives reimbursement for client services only after substantial outlays. Even monthly reimbursement schedules usually require substantial lines of credit at local financial institutions. The personal homes that clinic managers often must put up as collateral make more concrete the monetary value of these lines of credit. In addition, home equity loans may be foregone by the managers whose homes and other property already are tied up in lines of credit. The difference between the costs of these home equity loans and other loans is a very real cost of obtaining a line of credit as is any interest paid to maintain loans under the line of credit. These costs should be distributed using the methods adopted for other overhead costs. To compare costs of programs that operate in different economic climates or to compare publicly funded versus privately funded programs, the same interest rate might be used in assessing the cost of financial resources (if, in fact, one wishes to control for disparities in local financing costs).

Protection From Financial Risks: Insurance

Insurance is an additional expense that purchases a less intangible but still highly valuable commodity: protection from risk of excessive financial liability. Insurance can include property insurance, professional liability insurance, life and disability insurance, and coverage for physical injuries experienced by staff and clients alike on service system premises. These expenses usually can be taken at face value and distributed over clients as other overhead costs are distributed. If the program being assessed carries no insurance, it may be covered by affiliates. If the organization being assessed is self-insured, monthly payments to insurance accounts can be used or one can resort to rates for comparable insurance on the open market.

Transportation

Certainly, transportation provided to clients needs to be included in cost assessment. If a client drives or is driven to a service site to receive one particular procedure, such as day care or legal advice on separation, the cost of transportation should be assigned to that procedure only. The published federal or another agreed-on rate of cost per unit distance (e.g., 32¢ per mile) can be used to figure the cost exactly. If standard rates for transportation are not used, vehicle maintenance, insurance, and related expenses (e.g., gasoline, oil, taxes, registration) need to be added to annual depreciation figures to reflect total vehicle expenses.

If vehicles or transportation funds are used by counselors for community outreach, the cost can be allocated to a specific procedure (outreach) and distributed over the clients for whom outreach was performed. Transportation expenses by managers and similar personnel may not be allocable to any one procedure or client and thus need to be distributed over all in the same manner as the time of overhead personnel is distributed.

Other Resources Expended
as a Result of Services Rendered

Although the categories described earlier constitute the major resources consumed in provision of most health and human services, it always is advisable to ask all interested parties if additional resources are being used. Unlike outcome assessment, which often misses some of the results of treatment but nevertheless is viewed as valid, a cost assessment that misses significant costs has underreported service expenditures and thus is inadequate and invalid.

Taking a more societal perspective on cost assessment, it is not only the clinics and clients who pay for human services. Community residents, for example, may experience lower property values and lower home-selling prices as residential treatment facilities become established or as deinstitutionalized patients establish impromptu residence in neighborhood parks. Although regrettable and often caused by unwarranted fears, these drops in property value can affect the lives of community residents in very material ways, including loss of real estate investment, lower selling prices for homes, and lower home equity loans. Declines in property value that are attributable to provision of a human service may not be popular with some interest groups but, for a complete accounting of program costs, they need to be distributed over clients and procedures as are expenditures of overhead resources. These are but some of the many possible additional costs of service programs about which cost assessment should inquire. Inquiries should be directed to parties involved in treatment procedures or affected by treatment outcomes.

ISSUES IN MEASURING
AND MONITORING RESOURCE USE

We have discussed the basic procedures for and nuances of the assessment of the value of resources consumed in human service organizations. It would seem that we have gotten pretty specific about how cost data are collected. There is much more to it, however. For instance, when discussing

the "nitty-gritty" of cost assessment, a major concern is the cost of collecting, compiling, and analyzing data on costs.

Sampling in Cost Assessment

The cost assessor's choice of the period over which cost data are
collected and of the persons, places, procedures, and other resources that
are valued for cost can make a big difference in the final cost figures.
Ideally, cost data are collected over the entire duration of service operations
for all clients and all change agents. One reason for this is the need for large
sample sizes to conduct the inferential statistical analyses, such as multiple
regression, that allow isolation of the program procedures responsible for
therapeutically meaningful changes in client processes and outcomes.
Another rationale for 100% sampling is to assure representativeness. If cost
data were gathered over only a few months out of the year, the sort of
seasonal variations common in services could produce serious underesti-
mations or overestimations of cost. If cost data were collected for a subset
of counselors or clients, the subset might not be representative. The most
efficient counselors might be chosen for a one-time evaluation, for example. For ongoing evaluation formats such as CPPOA, however, it is more
likely that close monitoring would focus on counselors whose time use was
a matter of some concern. Similarly, clients whose treatment was most
straightforward and whose cases were deemed most representative by
certain interest groups might be the only cases for which cost data were
collected. All these missampling procedures could generate erroneous
conclusions.

It is, of course, possible to obtain data of any sort from representative
samples if the population from which the sample is drawn is so large that
a sample would be adequate for whatever statistical analyses were planned
in the CPPOA (and if obtaining data for the whole population would be
prohibitively expensive). Power analyses (Bloom, 1995; Cohen, 1965,
1988, 1990) can determine the sample size logically and quickly. Software
developed by Dallal (1988) and others allows calculations of sample size
for a variety of designs under a number of different assumptions. Experience conducting CPPOA and other research in a variety of human service
systems suggests, however, that the total population of clients seen over
several years is barely adequate for simple program evaluation. Full-
fledged CPPOA is more demanding.

Supposing that a client population of sufficient size exists, sampling
could be used to control research costs when obtaining data on costs and
the other classes of variables (i.e., outcomes, procedures, processes) for

CPPOA. The sample would be selected using the same careful procedures for constructing a representative sample that have been developed by social scientists (e.g., Fox, 1986; Jaeger, 1984; Rea, 1992). Health insurance claims databases could be used as a source of data for costs and procedures if the claims accurately represent the types and values of resources consumed and the procedures performed. It would be essential, of course, to collect data on procedures, processes, and outcomes, as well as on costs, for the same clients. Repeated data collection could change the procedures and alter the processes for these agents and clients, naturally; that always is a risk in applied research. In sampling studies, there could be some intensification of this reactivity due to the heightened concern of researchers to collect data on all variables from the clients selected by the sampling algorithms. The magnitude of this reactivity, and its beneficial or inhibitive nature, could be assessed by comparing the sampled clients to other clients on unobtrusive or routinely collected measures. For example, the duration of stay in a hospital could be compared for patients who were and were not selected for a study of the cost-benefit of surgery preparation. It is likely, however, that a sampling approach still would yield data of better quality at lower cost when large populations are available.

Estimation Versus Observation

Another strategy for controlling the costs of collecting data on costs and other CPPOA variables is *estimation* rather than observation of the costs, procedures, processes, and outcomes. This is attractive in its low cost but provides many opportunities for reducing the quality of cost data collected. The most gross form of estimation—guessing—probably is not what most people have in mind when they propose estimation of cost and other data. Carefully structuring estimates to elicit *worst case, best case,* and *most likely* values is more likely to yield meaningful information.

Estimation may be the only strategy available in some analyses for boiling down accounting records of total pay plus benefits to the cost of treating each client using each major procedure. Suppose an analysis must be performed on a program that already has collected all the outcome data to be used and that cost is included as an afterthought. Only accounting record data may be available for change agents, and no data may be available for temporal resources devoted by clients to treatment. To allocate agent time among clients and procedures, agents can be asked to estimate the amount of time spent with the average client on each major procedure, recording their estimates in matrices similar to those described earlier for recording the actual amount of time spent in these activities. In some cases, agents could be asked to provide these estimates for each client separately. Clients for whom they could not recall specific information could be given an average time value for each procedure. Interagent reliability could be examined by comparing reports of similar agents who worked with similar clients. The validity of agent reports could be tested by comparing estimates to observations of a few clients seen currently by the agents or, less optimally, clients seen at a similar service system. Simpler questionnaires could be developed to help clients estimate the amount of time spent in service-related activities, including transportation and homework time.

Of course, it is unlikely that the quality of cost data generated by estimation procedures will rival the quality of cost data that are collected with the same care, intensity, and comprehensiveness common in the collection of outcome data. There probably will be a trade-off between data quality and cost. After going below some level of data quality, it may be difficult to justify the collection of cost data by estimation.

Assessing Resource Constraints

The Nature of Temporal, Spatial, Material, and Other Constraints

Comprehensive measurement of resources consumed does not stop at assessment of value. To provide a quantitative basis for decisions about the allocation of limited resources among different service procedures, managers need to know exactly how limited each type of resource is. Resources that are valued in monetary units may have their limits described simply as whatever is indicated in the budget. Some temporal resources, such as the time that change agents can devote to different components of treatment, can be measured by looking up the budgets for each category of change agent personnel. Volunteers' time also needs to be assessed to ascertain the limits on temporal resources for change agents and other personnel. Client time is a particularly crucial resource that, in all but inpatient settings, is likely to be more limited than is sometimes thought (Yates, 1987). Employment imposes limits on client time that change agents recognize readily, but child care responsibilities and social activities may impose limits on time available for treatment activities even for unemployed clients.

More limiting than time or money available in budgets are the abilities of change agents. If staff cannot perform certain procedures due to lack of education, experience, or training, certain procedures that could be very effective will be impossible to implement. Although new capabilities can be added to a service system by changing personnel and by holding in-service workshops, these steps cause delays in procedure implementation and usually require additional funds. Staff also may resist training in new procedures. Thus, staff skills can additionally constrain the range of service procedures that can be used, independent of the time they have available. Spatial resources can impose additional, obvious constraints on the procedures that can be implemented and the number of clients who can be served. The number of offices in a college counseling center, for example, limits the number of clients who can be seen at any one time, and the presence and size of group meeting rooms affects the number of groups that can be held. Material resources, and the ability to access additional resources, may further limit the procedures that can be used.

What About Resources Consumed in Research?

Regular collection of data on resources, procedures, processes, and outcomes is part of the ongoing management of a human service system and can be considered a regular overhead cost. It may be useful to itemize costs of managerial data collection so that the cost-effectiveness and cost-benefit of collecting that data can be examined regularly. Intensive collection of data on particular relationships between new procedures, target processes and outcomes, and the resources required for these procedures, may be considered a research cost that is temporary and should be excluded from service costs. One problem with this formulation, however, is that what is *research* and what is *normal assessment* can be difficult to discern. This is especially likely in service programs that are established for the purposes of both conducting research and providing a health or human service. Also, the thorough assessment of costs (and of procedures, processes, and outcomes) that is typical of research efforts might improve the procedures, processes, and thus the outcomes of service (although clinical staff typically think the opposite). Excluding the costs of research would, in cases of positive reactivity, lead to underreporting of what it took to achieve the procedures, processes, and outcomes found in the rest of the CPPOA. Although resolution of this issue may be unique to each service system, I recommend collecting data on and reporting the costs of research per client per procedure.

Adjusting for Effects of Time and Duration of Assessment

Present Valuation Strategy

The temporal perspective on costs can affect cost totals significantly. The formula for calculating the present value of a stream of resource expenditures

Table 2.7

Present Values of Future Resource Expenditures
as a Function of Discount Rate

	Discount Rate				
	0.00	*0.02*	*0.04*	*0.06*	*0.08*
Year 1	1,000	980	962	943	926
Year 2	1,000	961	925	890	857
Year 3	1,000	942	889	840	794
Year 4	1,000	924	855	792	735
Year 5	1,000	906	822	747	681
Year 6	1,000	888	790	705	630
Year 7	1,000	871	760	665	583
Year 8	1,000	853	731	627	540
Year 9	1,000	837	703	592	500
Year 10	1,000	820	676	558	463
Total	10,000	8,983	8,111	7,360	6,710

NOTE: Values represent present-valuing monetized costs (in dollars) at different discount rates.

can be found as a built-in function on most business calculators and spreadsheet programs. Briefly, the most commonly used formula is

$$\sum_{y=1}^{z} \frac{\$_y}{(1 + d_y)^y}$$

where $\$_y$ is the cost of the service in time period (often 1 year) y of an evaluation spanning time periods 1 through z, and d_y is the discount rate for time period y.

The discount rate is chosen to be similar to the prime rate for the same period. The choice of discount rate can affect greatly the total present value of a long project, as shown in Table 2.7 for discount rates ranging from $d = .00$ to .08. One rule of thumb is to select a discount rate similar to the rate of interest that would have been earned by service system funds if they had been invested in a short-term financial instrument. Because the discount rate chosen can make such a difference in the final cost and may exacerbate or hide differences in cost between programs, present value assessments should be repeated for different discount rates (Thomas, 1971).

Calculating the present value of most streams of resource expenditures is not necessary in many CPPOAs because the period over which cost data are collected is simply too short (e.g., 6 months to 1 year). When the time period involves 2 or more years, and especially when interest rates are high (e.g., annual discount rates exceeding 10%), present value and other adjustments usually should be performed to keep cost data accurate and to provide more informative comparisons between alternative procedures or programs that differ in the resource expenditures they require early in the funding period.

Considering Inflation

Another situation that requires temporal adjustment so that all costs are expressed in common units is an analysis that incorporates data collected from several programs during different periods. For instance, the costs of a program in the early 1970s would have to be adjusted for inflation prior to comparison with the costs of a program in the mid-1990s. Inflation adjustment can be performed by first finding the rates of inflation for the health and human services sector for the region and years of data collection. To convert from earlier to later "dollars" (e.g., to 1997 dollars), the earlier costs would be multiplied by 1 plus the inflation rate during the year following the resource expenditure, and that result would be multiplied by 1 plus the inflation rate for the following year, until the final year (1997, in this instance) was reached.

The results of adjusting multiyear assessments of cost for inflation using this calculation procedure are shown in the rightmost column of Table 2.8. These contrast greatly with the results of simply totaling costs, as shown one column from the left. Of course, one can largely escape the need for any such adjustment of monetary values of resources if resources are valued in their native units (e.g., hours for temporal hours, square meters for spatial resources).

Multiple Perspectives on Costs

Opinions of different researchers and competing interest groups may vary on what types of resources should be included in cost assessments and what adjustments (e.g., for inflation, for present value) should be conducted on costs. If each perspective has merit, it may be preferable to report the findings of the cost assessment from each perspective separately. One ends up with not one but several bottom lines this way, but the result is more comprehensive. Recognizing the validity of each interest group's contribution to assessment also can avoid potentially destructive fights between or alienation of interest groups.

It is likely that one of the interest groups will advocate a cash perspective that equates cost with money spent, whereas another interest group will

Table 2.8

Effects of Inflation on Future Costs

Year	Cumulative "Raw" Cost of Program	Rate of Inflation That Year	Compounded Inflation	Cumulative Inflation-Adjusted Program Cost ($100,000/Year)
1	$100,000	0.07	1.07	$107,000
2	$200,000	0.09	1.17	$223,630
3	$300,000	0.11	1.29	$353,089
4	$400,000	0.10	1.42	$495,495
5	$500,000	0.08	1.54	$649,292
6	$600,000	0.07	1.65	$813,856
7	$700,000	0.07	1.76	$989,939
8	$800,000	0.04	1.83	$1,173,065
9	$900,000	0.06	1.94	$1,367,179
10	$1,000,000	0.05	2.04	$1,570,998

prefer to consider time, square footage, and whatever units are natural to the resource whose consumption is being assessed. One solution to disputes about which of these approaches to use is to report data and findings of analyses from each perspective and to see how different the results really are. Another solution is to see what orientation to resource assessment generates data that are most useful in analyzing and improving the relationships between treatment procedures, processes, and outcomes—the topics of the following chapters.

3

Monitoring Procedures, Processes, and Procedure → Process Relationships

Neither costs nor outcomes can be directly controlled by human service providers and scientist-manager-practitioners; only *procedures* can be controlled with any immediate degree of certainty. Performance of these procedures often is assumed but may be the source of program successes and failures. Even if procedures are implemented faithfully, the failure to attain targeted outcomes still cannot be understood unless the social, psychological, or biological processes that were supposed to be altered by the procedures can be shown to have occurred. To enable more complete understanding of what the service does with its resources and why those service procedures may fail to result in achievement of goal outcomes, this chapter explores key concepts and techniques for measuring procedures, processes, and the strength of procedure → process relationships.

CONCEPTUALIZING PROCEDURES AND PROCESSES IN HUMAN SERVICES

Procedures and Processes: What Service Providers Do and Inspire

The procedures of a human service are the observable actions of therapists, counselors, physicians, educators, nurses, social workers, and other agents of change—what they do and say. Physical actions, verbal exchanges, therapeutic drug administrations, and nonverbal postures and inflections all are part of the practice and art of delivering human services. The choice of procedures may be guided by theory, experience, legal statutes, or the simple faith that what has worked before will be likely to work again for similar clients. In any case, the procedures chosen are used because they are likely to change certain psychological, sociological, economic, or other processes that should, according to the hypotheses of the change agent, make the desired outcomes of the program more probable.

Medical and other health-related procedures are designed to modify physiological processes, such as high blood pressure, or psychological processes, such as depression. Psychological procedures, such as reflection and empathy, may nurture positive self-regard, whereas other procedures may be performed to elicit and eventually resolve anger about events in one's childhood. Groups might be designed to evoke the processes of observational learning from persons who have successfully coped with the death of a loved one. Training procedures for mentally retarded clients may target specific behavior routines that clients are supposed to acquire via systematic shaping and reinforcement.

Other procedures are not designed so much to evoke changes in processes as they are to facilitate delivery of other procedures. For instance, training parents to use behavioral techniques for managing their children is one type of procedure; *where* the training is conducted (e.g., individually or in groups; in clinic offices or in homes) is another type of procedure (Siegert & Yates, 1980). The former type of procedure can be called an *intervention procedure;* the latter might be termed a *delivery procedure.* Both intervention and delivery procedures determine whether critical physiological, psychological, and other processes occur, increase, continue, diminish, or cease in clients.

How Understanding Procedure → Process Relationships Can Reduce Costs or Improve Effectiveness

It is tempting to measure only whether specific procedures were performed and to assume that the psychological and other processes that were supposed to change as a result of those procedures did in fact change (and in the desired direction). This, however, is risky. Not examining the links between procedures and processes can result in missed opportunities to reduce costs or to devote resources to more effective procedures. Costs can be cut without decrements in outcome if the service system stops using procedures that do not change targeted processes. Understanding relationships between procedures and processes also can improve outcomes and avoid increases in service costs because resources that were devoted to ineffectual procedures now can be allocated to more immediate or more thorough implementation of procedures that have been found to affect key processes. For example, an academic counselor who had been spending time enhancing a personality characteristic in his students could devote the same time to training his students in a specific method for learning more from written materials (e.g., the SQ3R method researched by Robinson, 1970). Furthermore, if the targeted processes (e.g., increased self-esteem through positive imagery of achievement) were attained, even if the procedures that were supposed to achieve those processes were not implemented, it may be useful to know this. The procedures that were responsible for the outcomes might then be discovered.

Of course, it may be that the procedures performed by providers do have positive effects on some processes but that these changes simply were not detected because of poor measures for known processes or because unknown but powerful processes were in effect. Unmeasured processes may be crucial in attaining the desired outcomes. This can be discovered by measuring additional processes and then examining the relationship between the suspect procedures, the newly measured processes, and important outcomes. Alternatively, one could temporarily stop performing the supposedly unnecessary procedures for a randomly selected subset of clients and then note whether outcomes declined or not. Careful monitoring of outcomes could minimize harm to clients if the procedures proved necessary after all.

Useful, potentially cost-reducing information also is obtained if treatment procedures do change the targeted processes but the desired outcomes still are not attained. For example, if self-efficacy for delaying gratification is successfully improved but clients in an eating disorder program continue to binge, perhaps self-efficacy or delaying gratification are not important processes to alter for most clients. Last, it may be useful to know whether unattained processes coincide with the absence of change in procedures. This finding could mean that the approach (i.e., the procedure → process links focused on by the program) is viable but that program procedures are not being implemented correctly.

Resistances to Measuring Procedure → Process Relationships

If measuring these procedure → process linkages is such a good idea, though, why isn't it done in all evaluations? Possible reasons include the following:

- Some evaluators are uncertain as to what specific procedures are being followed by the service system(s) being studied (and are reluctant to ask or are not informed by the service systems).
- The particular psychological, sociological, biological, and economic processes that are supposed to be instilled or altered by service procedures are unknown or not agreed on by researchers, change agents, clients, or funders.

- The costs of measuring these procedures and processes would be excessive (e.g., either insufficient time or funds were budgeted for the evaluation or discord could be created among interest groups if research did not substantiate links between particular procedures, processes, or outcomes that have deep significance for an interest group).
- It is assumed that it is impossible to measure procedures, processes, or the relationships between them.

In particular, some care providers may perceive that they have little to gain and much to lose if the particular psychological, biological, or social processes on which their service procedures focus are not found to be influenced by program procedures. Other providers, managers, and even evaluators may not have based their provision, management, or evaluation of services on any specific theory, but instead on what is standard and customary. Theory-driven evaluation, like theory-driven practice and administration, attempts to increase the likelihood that procedures and processes will be assessed in human service evaluation by challenging assumptions about the difficulty of measuring procedures, processes, and their relationships (Bickman, 1987; Bickman, Hedrick, & Rog, 1993).

APPROACHES TO ASSESSING HUMAN SERVICE PROCEDURES AND PROCESSES

Investigating Procedures at Different Levels of Specificity

Procedures can be measured and managed (i.e., evaluated and adjusted to optimize outcomes and costs) at dramatically different levels of specificity. Many evaluations consider each treatment program to be a different single procedure. An entire mental health clinic, for example, might be compared to another mental health clinic or entire schools of therapy could be pitted against one another without examining the more specific effects of the various procedures used in the clinics or approaches (e.g., Sloane, Staples, Cristol, Yorkston, & Whipple, 1975). The macroprocedures of treating depression with either therapy, drugs, or a combination of the two has been assessed for effectiveness, although not for differences in cost (Elkin, Parloff, Hadley, & Autry, 1985). Comparison of macroprocedures on measures of cost and effectiveness probably is best conducted by implementing the procedures at a variety of sites with different change agents and client populations as was done in the national clinical trial for

treatments for depression (Elkin et al.). The results of analyzing macroprocedures can be used by state and federal officials and policymakers to
manage human services on a global scale (e.g., to assess the effectiveness,
cost-effectiveness, and cost-benefit of psychotherapy as a whole; Office of
Technology Assessment, 1980; Smith, Glass, & Miller, 1980; Yates &
Newman, 1980a, 1980b).

Mesolevels and *microlevels* of specificity also can be used to measure
procedures and to relate those procedures to specific processes, outcomes,
and costs. Within a program and even within the services provided by one
change agent, experimental and quasi-experimental designs can be used to
measure the relationships between different procedures and processes,
outcomes, and costs (Barlow, Hayes, & Nelson, 1984; Cook & Campbell,
1979; Jayaratne & Levy, 1979; Kazdin, 1982, 1992). Although aggregating
data over agents and programs may provide a clearer and more generalizable picture of relationships between costs, procedures, processes, and
outcomes, there are advantages to studying the relationships between these
variables within one's own practice or service system. One often can find
the particular procedures that work best in one's own setting with the clients
one typically sees.

Studying Processes at Different Levels of Specificity

Just as procedures can be described, understood, and managed at different levels of specificity, so can processes. Many processes are rooted to a
certain level of specificity. For example, although it is possible to describe
collective psychological processes at macrolevels (e.g., Jung, 1965; Marcuse, 1964), most psychological processes seem to occur at mesolevels and
microlevels in small groups and more often within the individual (Carver
& Scheier, 1981; Kuhl, 1985; for depression, see Haaga, Dyck, & Ernst,
1991). Alienation, depression, and empowerment all are processes that
occur within the individual and that can be addressed by procedures
enacted by therapists and community psychologists (e.g., Fairweather &
Davidson, 1986; Rounsaville et al., 1986). Biological processes can be
conceptualized at societal and community macrolevels (e.g., social prohibitions of abortion, chemical pollution of a bay) but also operate at an
individual level. There is strong evidence that even treatment procedures
not designed to effect biological processes can have measurable and
usually positive effects on psychological and biological variables. For
example, in a carefully controlled experiment, Bandura, Cioffi, Taylor, and
Brouillard (1987) found that patient use of psychological (i.e., cognitive)
strategies for coping with pain produced both positive changes in specific

self-efficacy expectancies regarding pain tolerance and releases of chemicals that the body uses to blunt pain (i.e., endogenous endorphins). Other methods of pain tolerance tested by Bandura et al. did not produce these cognitive and physiological effects.

Some macrolevel processes, such as the health of the local, national, and international economy, also can moderate processes and even outcomes of services. Gaining employment, for example, may be an important measure of the success of Job Club programs (Azrin, Philip, Thienes-Hontas, & Basalel, 1980) but may be more difficult in periods or locales experiencing economic difficulty. Political processes potentially subsume all other processes, although these are perhaps the most challenging to quantify and study as results of service procedures and as moderators of service outcomes and costs. Nevertheless, some service procedures are designed to produce changes in political as well as psychological processes. Consider, for instance, feminist therapy (e.g., Linehan & Wagner, 1990) and programs tailored to raising the consciousness of drug abusers about how drug use may perpetuate oppression.

Choosing the Processes to Assess
by Examining the Procedures Used

The Role of Theory in Studying
Procedure → Process Links

Ask a therapist, counselor, or other change agent what is done during contact with a client and the reply usually will refer to specific techniques that often involve observable and unobservable events. When queried about treatment procedures used and processes focused on, a cognitive-behavioral change agent might remark, "Well, we worked toward the outcome of maximum normal living by using that participant modeling procedure you showed us last week to alleviate her social anxiety at dances." An analyst might say,

> We explored his feelings about his father and stepfathers, with the hope of eventually resolving his ambivalence about his mother. This, in turn, should allow the patient to move beyond his adolescent behavior patterns and act in a manner more appropriate to the middle-aged man that he is.

What can be observed here, however, is that a meeting of agent and client occurred and that a verbal interaction of the agent and client ensued. The content of the interaction could be observed or recorded to verify that participant modeling was implemented or that the father and stepfathers were discussed. Beyond that, though, what is described as procedure by the change agent might be better considered in the realm of process (which also can be measured).

The link between procedure and process is usually indicated first by hunches and theories and later, it is hoped, by research findings and statistical test results. Often implicit in change agents' descriptions of their procedures is the theory that guides their efforts. In the latter example, the client's feelings about his father might be presumed to be responsible for subsequent regression to adolescent behaviors, such as rebelling against authority, which might be responsible for some decline in job performance. Furthermore, it may be hoped that by talking about his feelings, the client would be able to resolve conflicts about his father that might also clear up some feelings about his mother and lift the regression to adolescence. Or a different change agent might say regarding work with a middle-aged woman, "I reviewed with her the basic methods of assertion and rehearsed three different, likely confrontations between the client and her spouse." In both cases, hypotheses held by the change agent point to processes in the client that should be altered following execution of the procedure.

Psychological and Biological Processes

Other changes in the behaviors, cognitions, affect, or physiology of the client can be conceptualized as processes, too. A client might be advised to change his or her intake of caffeine by moving the time of the last cup of coffee to successively earlier hours of the evening (a procedure), to reduce caffeine levels later in the evening (a change in a biological process), to reduce sleep latency (an outcome). A counselor might spend considerable time teaching the client to recognize drinks and foods that can contain caffeine and related stimulants. The change agent might even work out a schedule for gradually decreasing caffeine intake and help the client adapt the schedule to his or her circumstances. All of these actions on the part of the counselor are procedures, but what happens within the client as a result of the procedure are processes. If the client has actually learned what foods contain caffeine and similar substances, a cognitive process has occurred. Knowledge has been instilled and, most likely, the constructive process of *self-monitoring* (e.g., Jarrett & Nelson, 1987; Richman, Riordan, Reiss, Pyles, & Bailey, 1988) has begun, both as results of the program procedure. If the client actually decreases caffeine intake, that behavior probably is best considered not a process (because it is outside the skin of the client, technically); instead, it is an interim outcome. Decreased caffeine intake is not the final outcome, of course. The long-term (or terminal) outcome is reserved for the goal of therapy—in this case, reduced latency to sleep onset.

Psychological processes may have a serial nature that can interact positively or negatively with treatment procedure depending on where the individual is in the phases of the process. For example, Prochaska, DiClemente, and Norcross (1992) describe how the outcomes of weight loss, smoking cessation, and other treatments may be determined largely by an interaction of the procedures used and the stage of readiness-to-change at which the client begins treatment. Programs designed for clients at one stage of change (e.g., the action stage) were found to be much less effective for clients who, prior to treatment, had shown that they were at an earlier stage of readiness-for-change (e.g., precontemplation). Prochaska et al. used specific measures of psychological processes occurring within clients to show how different service procedures (e.g., consciousness raising, counterconditioning, stimulus control, self-liberation, reinforcement management) had different effects for clients who were at different stages of readiness-for-change.

Social Processes

Processes that result from human service procedures can include changes within others with whom the client works or resides. Each process may instigate additional changes that can benefit primary, secondary, or tertiary clients. For example, a counselor's referral of a client to an employer might result in a part-time job. That job could increase a client's income, thus enabling him or her to rent a small apartment and boost self-esteem, both of which could reduce the likelihood that he or she would continue living with an abusive spouse. Some less desirable processes also might occur, such as a modest increase in guilt felt by the client. All of these processes could be attributed largely to the counseling procedure implemented by the counselor. Each process may in turn contribute to the attainment of outcomes that benefit society, such as decreased physical abuse, lower health expenses, and possibly fewer disturbed children.

Another example of the social processes that may be caused by service procedures is the reduction in stress and increase in productivity that can result from offering stress management procedures to a single person in an organization. Manuso (1978, 1981) estimates that for each individual receiving successful biofeedback and associated treatments for excessive stress, an average of five additional individuals with whom the treated individual works experience significant reduction in stress. This positive contagion of beneficial processes may be even more significant when organizational leaders receive treatment services.

Societal, Economic, and Political Processes

Last, some processes that affect outcomes may not be the result of treatment procedures at all. Ongoing issues, problems, and other biological, psychological, and social processes can interact with treatment procedures to enhance, diminish, or completely overwhelm the effects of human service procedures. For example, despite the best treatment for substance abuse, a client developing AIDS may continue to abuse some drugs that provide relief from pain, AIDS drug side effects, and thoughts of suicide. Also, being a single teenage mother without family support can evoke negative psychological processes. And, sometimes the support of a loving family member can combine with regular therapy to produce a dramatic return to normal functioning. For these reasons, processes considered extraneous by some interest groups—such as social support, health status, and economic self-sufficiency—may be important to measure in addition to targeted processes.

METHODS FOR MEASURING PROGRAM PROCEDURES

Assessing Standardized Procedures

Many of the procedures used in a human service system may be described in program procedure manuals or may be otherwise made explicit. Some services, such as intermediate care facilities for mentally retarded adults, are required to closely follow procedures that have been specified in great detail. Some service systems do not delineate their methods in any standardized, clear fashion. Operations of these service systems can be observed, and the procedures seen can be defined in a manner that allows others to recognize execution of a specific procedure. Following this, use of a specific procedure can be recorded by change agents, by clients, or can be noted by persons watching actual or videotaped sessions or listening to tapes of sessions as detailed later. It may be useful to do the same, at least for a brief period, in systems that have detailed operations manuals. Experience suggests that there is a natural drift from procedures planned by program directors and therapy supervisors to procedures used by persons who work directly with clients.

Table 3.1

Sample Monitoring Form for Procedure Implementation
for Intermediate Care Facilities for the Mentally Retarded

Quality Assurance Committee Monitoring Sheet
Implementation of Service Procedures per Client
Institute for Behavior Resources
Site: Jefferson Boulevard
July 199_ (7/1/9_ through 7/31/9_)

Procedure *(individual responsible)*	Clients			
	Bill *0453*	*Janet* *0187*	*John* *1110*	*Gertrude* *0045*
Home facilities				
Pharmacy (registered nurse)	Y N	Y N	Y N	Y N
Safety (maintenance)	Y N	Y N	Y N	Y N
Safety (home supervisor)	Y N	Y N	Y N	Y N
Sanitation (home supervisor)	Y N	Y N	Y N	Y N
. . .	. . .	. . .	. . .	. . .
Nonmedical services				
QMRP supervision	Y N	Y N	Y N	Y N
Social work liaison	Y N	Y N	Y N	Y N
Psychological services	Y N	Y N	Y N	Y N
. . .	. . .	. . .	. . .	. . .

SOURCE: Adapted from Filipczak and Yates (1989) and Yates and Filipczak (1989).
NOTE: Y = Yes: procedure performed; N = No record of procedure performance. This form was designed to be used with information gathered from client records.

Although recording each operation as it occurs may generate the most accurate and complete record, a sampling procedure can yield data for purposes of basic monitoring and possibly for CPPOA. Nonparticipants (neither clients nor change agents) can use structured checklists, as shown in Table 3.1, to record signs of execution of procedures ranging from setting water temperature correctly to dealing with client outbursts during or following visits to service facilities.

Of course, recording a few procedures on a single sheet of paper is unlikely to capture quantitatively the critical procedures used by the service system. Also, having a single person provide data on procedures or any other aspect of a service may provide a limited and biased perspective. Particular interactions between the data collector, clients, and change agents also may bias findings. Furthermore, one-time assessment of use of prescribed procedures by persons not perceived to be aligned with the service program may be resisted or data may be falsified. This is likely

Table 3.2

Sample Monthly Report of Procedure Implementation for
an Intermediate Care Facility for the Mentally Retarded (ICF-MR)

Quality Assurance Committee Report
Implementation of Service Procedures per Site by Percentage
Institute for Behavior Resources
July 199_ (7/1/9_ through 7/31/9_)

Procedure (individual responsible)	ICF-MR Facilities			
	Jefferson Boulevard	Randolph Avenue	Elton Court	Mean for Homes
Home facilities				
Pharmacy (registered nurse)	73	100	100	91
Safety (maintenance)	88	100	88	92
Safety (home supervisor)	75	100	100	92
Sanitation (home supervisor)	78	97	100	92
Average over items	81	98	97	92
Nonmedical services				
QMRP supervision	83	no data	97	90
Social work liaison	100	no data	100	100
Psychological services	75	no data	50	87
. . .	. . .	. . .	. . .	. . .

SOURCE: Adapted from Filipczak and Yates (1989) and Yates and Filipczak (1989).
NOTE: This form was designed to be used with information gathered from client records.

when noncompliance with service procedures can result in sanctions, lawsuits, and loss of funding.

The degree to which different service procedures are used probably is best recorded by multiple observers who visit facilities or observe sessions at different times and who record a range of procedures with which they are familiar. The result can be a regular (e.g., monthly) report of where different parts of a service system are on continua reflecting more or less complete implementation of prescribed services procedures (e.g., Table 3.2).

Implementation of specific procedures during individual or group sessions can be assessed by making audio or video tapes of the session. Raters who have been trained to acceptable levels of validity and reliability then can listen to or watch the tapes. Occurrence of each service procedure can be noted as it is implemented, using checkoff or rating systems, as shown in Table 3.3. Procedure data can be collected independently from a number of raters to maintain validity. A subset (say, 10%) of the tapes can be assessed independently by various pairs of raters to assess reliability.

Table 3.3

Recording Form for Counseling Procedure Implementation

Counseling Session Procedure Monitoring

Client:
Change Agent:
Date of Session:

Component for Second Session, Individual Counseling	Implemented?		Degree of Procedure Implementation		
1. Greeting	No	Yes	Minimal	Basic	Complete
Problem review					
2. Review of first presenting problem	No	Yes	Minimal	Basic	Complete
3. Review of second presenting problem	No	Yes	Minimal	Basic	Complete
4. Review of additional presenting problems	No	Yes	Minimal	Basic	Complete
Goal operationalization					
5. Operationalization of client goals for first problem	No	Yes	Minimal	Basic	Complete
6. Operationalization of client goals for second problem	No	Yes	Minimal	Basic	Complete
7. Operationalization of client goals for additional problems	No	Yes	Minimal	Basic	Complete
Education					
8. Basic problem solving	No	Yes	Minimal	Basic	Complete
9. Self-management via reinforcement	No	Yes	Minimal	Basic	Complete
10. Cognitive self-management	No	Yes	Minimal	Basic	Complete
Next time					
11. Review goals for client homework	No	Yes	Minimal	Basic	Complete
12. Confirm time and date of next session	No	Yes	Minimal	Basic	Complete

NOTE: Consult *Program Procedure Guidelines Handbook* for operationalizations of each procedure.

Reliability can be maximized by not telling the raters which tapes will be checked for agreement. Validity can be monitored by occasionally having a criterion rater also listen to or watch the tapes. Details on maximizing reliability and validity of observation procedures are provided by Bass (1987) and Johnson and Bolstad (1973; see also Jorgensen, 1989; Teegarden & Burns, 1993; Zuardi, Loureiro, & Rodrigues, 1995).

Nonparticipants need not be the sole providers of data on the execution of service procedures: Often, agents and clients can do so as well. Chapter 2 described how the cost of each procedure could be assessed by having clients or therapists report each delivery of the procedure. The forms described there (see Yates et al., 1993) allowed both change agents and primary clients to record the occurrence of treatment procedures and their durations along with the resources involved in the procedure.

Assessing Procedures Not Standardized

If the procedures of a service system are not standardized, procedures can be recorded as they occur, and the commonalities among procedures can be discerned later via statistical or other analyses.

Subjective Determination of Program Procedures

If data collection resources (including available time and expertise) are limited, an alternative approach to operationalizing program procedures is to hold a series of meetings with staff members and their supervisors and ask them to develop procedure definitions and a data collection instrument. Beneficial side effects of these meetings often include improvement of services and easier administration of the service system. Increased consensus regarding what is supposed to be done when, to whom, by whom, and for what purpose can reeducate and remotivate staff. I have held similar meetings to operationalize program outcomes and costs. Several cycles of discussion, drafting of concrete items and administration procedures, and feedback from staff and administrators were necessary. The instruments that were developed did demonstrate reliability and discriminative validity (Davis & Yates, 1982; Yates et al., 1979). The following sections describe strategies for these procedure and process operationalization meetings and what can be done after the meetings reach consensus.

Empirical Determination of Procedure Use

To collect data on an unknown set of program procedures, one basically develops a program procedures manual according to what is actually done in the program. This usually requires observation of clients to record whatever procedures occur, either in live observation sessions or via audiotape or videotape. One begins by listing all possible agents, clients, and actions that agents can perform with clients. The level of specificity at which actions are described, and terms used, are likely to be dictated by the theoretical approach favored by the service system. For example, after observing the operation of a commercial program to help minimize the effect on productivity of stricter smoking prohibitions, evaluation agents might develop different lists of what they thought to be the principle components of the program. These lists could then be reconciled, compared to what program staff consider the major parts of the program, and CPPOA could proceed.

A more intensive, empirical method of "componentizing" a program would be to observe and record the particulars of services received by individual clients. In a residential program for problem children, for example, teams of observers might use clipboards or handheld microcomputers to record each episode of delivery of each discrete service procedure. Initially, the observation system might need to record all events that might or might not be planned service procedures. After observing a previously designated client for a set period of time (e.g., 30 seconds), an observer might describe each event that had occurred during the period in a sentence format, by checking off the appropriate subject phrase, action phrase, object phrase and descriptive phrase. For example, as shown in Figure 3.1, the occurrence of a child angrily hitting a staff member is recorded for the third time period by checking the subject phrase *Child,* the action phrase *Fight,* the object phrase *Staff (Teaching Parents),* and the descriptive phrase *Angrily.* The end of the time period can be indicated by a beep from a timer if tapes are being observed or by a beep in an observer's earphone if clients are being observed live.

Another approach to recording the implementation of specific procedures is to record the behaviors of the client and then to record what preceded and followed those behaviors. In many programs, a critical component of treatment is structuring the response that other people make to the client's behavior. These consequences, and what may have led to the client's behavior (the antecedents), can be recorded using an antecedent → behavior → consequence (ABC) format (Table 3.4). More structured instruments for collecting data on the use of different program procedures may be developed after a period of recording procedures in the ABC format.

Once these specific procedures have been recorded for a number of clients and agents over a significant period of time, particular patterns of procedure administration may be discernible. Change agents, and possibly secondary and even primary clients, can be asked to cluster procedures

Learning House

2.09, BTY 9/24/73

Observation Sheet

Date:	Time Intervals: (1 minute each)	0	1	2	3	4	5	...	60
___/___/___	SUBJECT PHRASES								
Day of Week (circle one):	Child				✓				
M Tu W Th F	Staff (Teaching Parents)								
Sa Su	Parental Guardian								
	[continued]								
Time of Day Observed:	ACTION PHRASES								
___:___ ___M	Adding up points								
to	Cry								
___:___ ___M	Doing homework								
Observer's Name Code:	Eat								
	Fight				✓				
	[continued]								
Observation Site(s):	OBJECT PHRASES								
	Child								
	Clothing								
Staff / Guardians Present:	Door								
	Furniture								
	Staff (Teaching Parents)				✓				
	[continued]								
Subject Name Code:	DESCRIPTIVE PHRASES								
	Alone								
Notes:	Angrily				✓				
	Arguingly								
	Braggingly								
	[continued]								

Figure 3.1. Process and Incident Reporting System

NOTE: [continued] denotes that additional items were present on the actual observation sheet.

using *conceptual mapping* (Trochim, 1989; Trochim & Linton, 1986; see also Cook, 1992; Kohler, 1993) or similar statistical manipulations. The results may help discern and measure specific service procedures, especially when the findings of conceptual mapping are integrated with theory regarding what procedures have been shown to affect what processes. These procedure clusters then may be measured with instruments that monitor a few procedures to represent the cluster.

Table 3.4

An Illustrative Antecedent-Behavior-Consequence (ABC) Chart

Number/Antecedent	Behavior	Consequence
1. 6:00 p.m., male teaching parent (TP) announces loudly with enthusiasm, "Dinner's ready; come and get it!"	Subject of observation (S) comes downstairs, approaches the dinner table.	Female TP asks S, "[name], have you washed your hands?"
2. (Preceding consequence)	S says to female TP, rudely, "Yes, this morning!," then turns the chair to face away from the table and sits down, resting chin on top of the chair back. Stares at female TP.	Male TP: "[S's name], that is inappropriate verbal behavior to a teaching parent: take out your card and take off 700 points."
3. (Preceding consequence)	S takes out card and pencil from hip pocket, marks "700" in Positive Points column. (!) S replaces card and pencil in pocket and proceeds to pick up knife and fork and cut fish fillet.	Female TP says, "[S's name], I'm glad you recorded those negative points so promptly, but you still need to wash your hands before eating dinner."

Automating Collection of Data on Service Procedures

Implementation of some service procedures can be recorded automatically. For example, Brady (1987) has developed a computerized system for methadone administration that not only looks up and mixes the scheduled dose but pumps the liquid into a cup for consumption by the patient. It then records each administration in a database along with notes from nurses and counselors. Other procedures can be recorded with minimum effort but in a way that allows pinpointing of the time, agent, and client involved. Checklists of standard procedures can be listed on forms or mark-sense sheets and checked off as the procedure is executed. Handheld computers could be programmed with menus of possible treatment procedures, agents, and clients that could be pulled down with the touch of a stylus. The appropriate procedure, agent, and client could be recorded and the procedure sequence stored in a database on the computer or sent via wireless network to another computer (e.g., a network server). By computerizing procedure data, they could be summarized and fed back to agents, managers, and other interested parties easily, inexpensively, readily, and regularly. Data on procedures, and on other types of data collected in CPPOA, can provide the basis for specific questions and recommendations for action during case conferences.

MEASURING BIOPSYCHOSOCIAL AND OTHER PROCESSES

There are several ways of capturing for study the biological, psychological, social, and economic processes that are produced by service procedures and that are active in determining program outcomes. The specific theories or hypotheses that were the basis for using the procedures of the program usually point to more or less specific processes that are supposed to be either initiated, decreased, increased, or maintained as a result of the procedures. The first steps in measuring these processes are to list the major service procedures and then to assign to each procedure one or more processes that are supposed to change as a result, as shown in Table 3.5. Processes listed here can include some that are initiated by changes in other processes, also shown in Table 3.5. Then one can choose specific measures for those processes that are supposed to change during service provision.

For example, as illustrated in Figure 3.2, the (a) procedure of providing child management training to the primary caretaker in homeless families may be hoped to evoke the processes of increased (b) knowledge of, (c) skills for, and (d) self-efficacy regarding the management of one's children plus (e) reduced anxiety about the psychological and physical well-being of one's children. Processes (b) through (d) in turn lead to both (f) more effective child rearing on the part of the parent and (g) reduced misbehavior on the part of the children. This last process also was augmented by the earlier process (e) of reduced anxiety, as is (h) reduced anger at the children. Processes (f), (g), and (h) all (i) reduce the risk that the children will be taken away from the homeless parent for foster care.

Use Standard Process Measures? Develop Your Own?

There is no simple answer for these questions. Methods for measuring prominent biological processes are reasonably standard, but methods for assessing psychological, social, and other processes altered by human services can be a very different matter. If there is a standard measure that

Table 3.5

Form for Recording Self-Reports of Processes (Expectancies)
That May Moderate Procedure → Outcome Relationships

Treatment Procedure	*Self-Efficacy Expectancy Rating*									
	I doubt very much that I can perform this procedure.							*I am very confident that I can perform this procedure.*		
1. Weekly group counseling	1	2	3	4	5	6	7	8	9	10
2. Cognitive transformations of tempting situations	1	2	3	4	5	6	7	8	9	10
3. Covert sensitization to tempting situations	1	2	3	4	5	6	7	8	9	10
. . .	. . .									
n (last procedure)	1	2	3	4	5	6	7	8	9	10
Treatment Procedure	*Compliance Expectancy Rating*									
	I doubt very much that I will perform this procedure.							*I am very confident that I will perform this procedure.*		
1. Weekly group counseling	1	2	3	4	5	6	7	8	9	10
2. Cognitive transformations of tempting situations	1	2	3	4	5	6	7	8	9	10
3. Covert sensitization to tempting situations	1	2	3	4	5	6	7	8	9	10
. . .	. . .									
n (last procedure)	1	2	3	4	5	6	7	8	9	10

SOURCE: Adapted from Williams and Yates (1993).

captures the crucial processes posited to the service system, I would use it. It is possible, however, that no standard measure exists for some of the processes posited to be crucial determinants of service outcomes. Available measures for psychological processes may be too lengthy, may contain scales for other processes of little interest to the evaluation, or may not be sufficiently reliable, valid, or sensitive to service-induced changes in processes.

It is relatively easy to design the first draft of an instrument to measure a psychological process. Also, staff may be more enthusiastic about, and more likely to continue reporting data for, a measure they have developed. The problems usually begin when the measure is used by clients. Problems of interpretation, readability, and scoring usually lead to low reliability and poor validity. The content of some items also may reduce reliability or validity or both. Several cycles of revision by staff and evaluators can hone

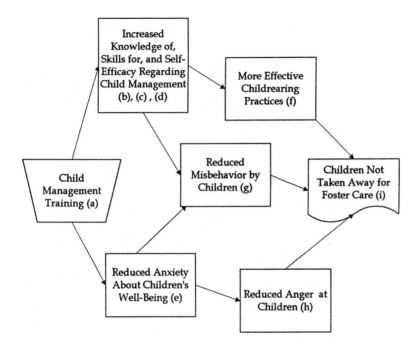

Figure 3.2. Sample Procedure → Process Links for Child Management Component of a Program for Homeless Families

the quality of a newly developed instrument but also may leave one wishing that a standard measure of known reliability and validity had been found and used from the beginning. Standardized measures also allow compilation of data on procedure → process relationships over different service programs and comparison of processes generated at different sites.

Questionnaires

For most psychological processes that have been hypothesized to contribute to treatment outcome, one or more instruments have been developed to detect the presence or absence of that process in an individual and often the magnitude or intensity of the process as well. Some instruments have become the object of intense research and development efforts. These measures generally are reliable, reasonably valid for most tasks, but also may have numerous scales and can be costly to administer. Comprehensive standardized instruments may well include scales for the particular processes under investigation, but they cannot be assumed to assess all the important psychological processes that may contribute to outcomes.

Usually, it is more efficient to scour the literature to find the most reliable, valid, and widely used instrument for assessing the specific processes of interest. Computerized searches of the relevant literature as abstracted in databases such as PsycINFO® in CD-ROM formats (e.g., PsychLIT®) or via inexpensive gateways, such as BRS After Dark®, can reveal what measures are used most often by investigators. Reliability and validity statistics also may be found in the literature. Some computerized databases are devoted entirely to summaries and critical reviews of measures of psychological, sociological, and related processes—for instance, the Mental Measurements Yearbook Database—that can be accessed on national commercial networks, such as CompuServe®. Local and university libraries (e.g., the Washington D.C. University Consortium's ALADIN) may offer access to extensive computerized databases, too.

Sometimes an investigator may be familiar enough with a literature that the measure of choice is clear, such as the Beck Depression Inventory (Beck, 1961) for depression. In other circumstances, a new measure may have to be developed from other measures. This often can be accomplished by adapting items from other measures, as was done historically with items from the Minnesota Multiphasic Personality Inventory (MMPI) to construct scales of anxiety, such as the Taylor Manifest Anxiety Scale (Taylor, 1953). Sometimes measures for all the hypothesized processes—and many of the targeted outcomes—are abbreviated and integrated into one long form. For example, the Individual Assessment Profile (Flynn, Hubbard, Forsyth, Fountain, & Smith, 1992) contains items assessing depression, drug use, living arrangements, health, sources of financial support, illegal activities, and treatment and arrest history. These instruments may be validated by demonstrating their ability to prediction client dysfunction or the outcomes of treatment (e.g., Flynn et al., 1995). Of course, once a subset of the items in a particular inventory is lifted out of its original context and placed next to items from other measures, reliability and validity need to be reassessed. This is rarely done; it should be done and need not take a great deal of time or effort.

Structured Interviews

Questionnaires do not always capture the processes responsible for program outcomes either because the incorrect process was measured or because the processes are not present in the situation in which question-naires are administered. For example, although Type A personality may be a psychological process important to the occurrence of coronary heart disease, it may not be measured accurately when one completes a question-naire for Type A personality (Booth-Kewley & Friedman, 1987). Only when one is challenged, such as by interruptions by an interviewer and by other intrusive or evaluative interactions, may the Type A personality emerge and be measurable (Booth-Kewley & Friedman, 1987). This may explain why research using the Structured Interview (SI) measure, with its interactive interview format, found that Type A personality was an impor-tant process in determining heart disease, whereas research using the Jenkins Activity Survey (JAS) questionnaire did not (Booth-Kewley & Friedman, 1987). These particular instruments also illustrate another point in process assessment. The JAS was chosen over the SI for a large-scale study because it cost less to administer, among other things. This excessive concern about cost may have diminished the usefulness of a large set of data.

Structured interviews are available for many processes, including psy-chological functioning and personality disorders (e.g., the Millon Clinical Multiaxial Inventory, Version II). Survey interviewing (Fowler, 1993; Fowler & Mangione, 1989) often is an excellent way to examine the effect of service procedures on biopsychosocial processes.

Biological Indicators

Biological measures of processes can include assays of the by-products of processes, such as stress and mood (e.g., saliva tests for IgA; Stone, Cox, Valdimarsdottir, Jandorf, & Neale, 1987; for addiction, see Willette, 1989), that are supposed to change when particular components of treatment are administered. Biological indicators also can be found for behavioral pro-cesses that were to change after services were delivered. For example, a community program for reducing high blood pressure might measure client compliance with a medication regimen by regular urine or tissue assays for chemical flags that were included in the medication. Crucial components of diet, such as cholesterol intake, can be monitored with blood tests for the consumed substances.

Self-Reports

Although questionnaires can be considered self-reports in a loose sense, some of the internal processes that are supposed to change as a result of human services are known only to the client and can be best assessed by regular reports from the client. These reports can be prompted with forms that are to be turned in weekly at counseling meetings, in daily phone calls from therapists or research assistants (Lavrakas, 1993; see also Davis & Yates, 1983), or in response to beeps from pagers or miniature computers that request a quick synopsis of one's present thoughts or a rating of one's current emotional status (Mahoney, 1991). Self-reports of cognitions, affects, or acts can be made in diarylike formats or on more organized forms that request specific antecedents and consequences for each response (Yates, 1985, 1986a). A variety of self-efficacy, outcome, difficulty, and compliance expectancies specific to program procedures and to biological, psychological, and social processes could be assessed to see which might mediate outcomes of substance abuse programs. Self-reports of self-efficacy expectancies often have been shown to be powerful moderators of the effect of therapeutic procedures on behavioral outcomes (Bandura, 1982; see also Bandura, Adams, & Beyer, 1977). Compliance expectancies also show promise in predicting outcomes of some treatments (Williams & Yates, 1993). Table 3.5 shows how Williams and Yates assess these and other (i.e., component-specific self-efficacy) expectancies.

Human service providers who have been lied to by clients are reluctant to consider self-reports of processes as reliable or valid. Certainly, clients will be motivated to falsify data when threatened with punishment for reporting undesirable acts or when asked to devote excessive time to complete self-report forms. Demand characteristics (Kazdin, 1992) also may foster false reports of the occurrence, modification, or cessation of cognitive or emotional processes that were supposed to change as a result of treatment procedures. Valid self-reports are more likely when process reports are given directly to researchers and when clients know that change agents never see process data for individual clients. In these circumstances, self-reports of behaviors, cognitions, and emotions often are the best predictors of future behavior (Kirigen, Braukmann, Atwater, & Wolf, 1977; Lasky et al., 1959; Mischel, 1965).

Often, self-reports are the only means of obtaining information about important processes that may moderate the relationship between outcomes and those procedures that were supposed to lead to the outcomes. For example, only the client may know how much depression he or she is feeling, how many invitations for drug use were resisted successfully, how much anger is being coped with, how many angina attacks were experienced, or how many times today he or she resisted an almost irresistible urge to have a drink.

The Role of Research in Selecting Process Measures

The best measures of processes will not help CPPOA if those processes do not, in fact, lead to the interim or long-term outcomes that are the focus of the service program. Reviewing the research on those process → outcome relationships that are hypothesized to be important for the program may be the best way to help evaluators discern what processes are and are not most important to measure (thus also helping to minimize costs of assessing processes). For some processes, research may show that the process thought to be related to outcome needs to be refined. In the case of Type A personality, for example, there is some evidence that the Type A behavior pattern is too broad a trait. Specific components of Type A, already measured by the SI (i.e., Potential for Hostility and Anger-In scales) seem to be responsible for the link between Type A personality and heart disease (Booth-Kewley & Friedman, 1987). Knowing this could not only help assessment of processes but also could help service managers better focus clinical efforts on changing Type A personality to reduce heart disease risk (Friedman et al., 1986).

Contributions of Nonspecific Procedures and Processes

A variety of theorists and researchers have suggested over the years that most outcomes in human services (particularly mental health programs) are the result of unspecified and possibly unspecifiable processes. Frank (1973, 1982), for example, has maintained that nonspecific treatment procedures are responsible for most of the effect of psychotherapy. Comprehensive reviews of relationships between different therapy procedures and the resulting processes and outcomes suggest that procedures common to most mental health services are responsible for as much as half of the effect of those services. This position has been buttressed with empirical support. In a meta-analytic summary of 475 studies of the effectiveness of psychological therapies, Smith et al. (1980) found that placebo therapy procedures designed to avoid the specifics of most schools of therapy were approximately half as effective as specific bona fide therapy procedures.

The Smith et al. findings suggest that nonspecific factors are discernible processes that facilitate outcomes and that deserve to be studied and eventually made specific (Parloff, 1986). Strupp and Hadley (1979), among others, have attempted to contrast the effect of nonspecific to specific procedures and processes. Other clinical researchers have investigated other possible elements of nonspecific factors, such as the relationship between outcomes and various processes inspired by interactions of patient and therapist characteristics (e.g., Fullerton, Yates, & Goodrich, 1990). Other researchers have shown that specific treatment procedures contribute significantly to outcomes above and beyond the contribution of nonspecific factors. Longo, Clum, and Yaeger (1988) found that, relative to groups that included many nonspecific procedures of therapy, applying specific treatment procedures reduced the frequency and severity of genital herpes eruptions (shedding). A nonspecific procedure in therapy tested by Longo et al. was discussion of interpersonal conflicts among herpes sufferers. Specific therapy procedures examined by Longo et al. were group training in stress management, relaxation, and imagery.

In the mental health research literature, there are numerous examples of this sort of procedure → process research and of process → outcome research. Usually these studies are labeled *process research,* not differentiating between procedures and processes. Most clinical trials and most so-called outcome research really examine only procedure → outcome or process → outcome relationships. In clinical trials, clients are assigned randomly to one of several alternative collections of procedures. The effects of these procedures on processes, or on interim or long-term outcomes, are then measured and reported. In other forms of process research, natural variations in the degree to which procedures are implemented are correlated with variations in processes and outcomes. This approach avoids the problems of random assignment but increases the number and plausibility of alternative explanations for whatever findings emerge (Kazdin, 1992).

The absence, in some areas, of consistent findings in the literature about which service procedures instill or alter which biopsychosocial processes and about which processes lead to desirable outcomes does not mean that procedures and processes cannot be studied within a service system or a community of service systems. Procedures can be measured and processes can be assessed during treatment for each client, provider, and program. Findings from this sort of procedure → process → outcome research can be fed back to the program so that only the processes most closely linked to outcomes are the focus of treatment procedures. The challenge in this research is to measure outcomes in a manner that allows them to be linked back to specific processes. That is the topic of the next chapter.

4

Evaluating Outcomes:
Effectiveness and Benefits

To provide a comprehensive picture of a human service system that will be valuable for program managers, practitioners, clients, funders, researchers, and other interest groups, the numerous outcomes of that service system need to be described and quantified. That is the topic of this chapter. Even the most carefully measured outcomes do not provide real understanding of the service system that can be the basis for real improvement. A complete formative evaluation includes measurement of the strength of relationships between outcomes and the processes that were supposed to produce the outcomes. Methods for qualitatively and quantitatively describing process → outcome relationships and other linkages between costs, procedures, processes, and outcomes are discussed in the next chapter.

CONCEPTS OF OUTCOMES

Experimental Design, Multiple Outcomes, and Reciprocal Determinism

What happens as a *result* of human service provision may be different from what happens *after* human service provision. When an improvement in a client is noticed, one always is mildly uncertain whether the procedures of treatment caused the improvement, whether procedures initiated outside treatment caused the improvement, or whether processes not affected by the procedures were responsible for the improvement. It is tempting to posit that any positive outcomes simply result from the program. Problems with this position are revealed, however, if the outcomes are found to be largely negative. Whereas desirable outcomes usually are uniformly attributed to program procedures, undesirable outcomes usually are blamed on factors extraneous to the program. The difficulty of maintaining these two positions simultaneously prompts most evaluators to evoke the advantages of systematically manipulating procedures to be more certain about the causes of different outcomes. As was the case with relationships between procedures and processes, coverage of research designs is beyond the scope of this book (Kazdin, 1992). It is assumed that the assessment of outcomes uses the strongest experimental design that is feasible and acceptable to the controlling interest groups.

Traditional evaluation research designs often take the position that the outcomes of a human service are analogous to the single dependent variable of a laboratory or field experiment and that the provision of services is analogous to manipulation of one or two independent variables (Campbell & Stanley, 1963; Cook & Campbell, 1979). Just as more contemporary approaches to program evaluation consider numerous procedures and processes (e.g., Guba & Lincoln, 1989; Posavac & Carey, 1989) so can outcomes be considered plural and diverse. The metaphor used in CPPOA is not the simple laboratory study but the complex web of causal linkages found in modern path-analytic studies of how human interactions affect subsequent behavior (e.g., Turner, Irwin, Tschann, & Millstein, 1993). According to this conceptual viewpoint, a program for homeless families is not a homogeneous entity but is diverse in its procedures, targeted processes, and hoped-for outcomes. This variety and complexity requires that multiple outcomes be measured, just as multiple procedures and processes were measured, to provide a more complete model of the service system. This variety of outcomes then can be reported as alternative views on the results of treatment procedures and the expenditures of service resources. It also may be possible to combine information on multiple measures of outcomes with different perspectives on outcomes to yield a single composite measure, as described later in this chapter.

Another assumption of classic experimental design is that the program procedures and the processes they address are the sole causes of program outcomes. Outcomes of human services usually are more complex in their etiology. Factors exogenous to the service system, such as gender, ethnicity, and economic circumstances, may inhibit or facilitate the effect of services. Using multiple regression and other analyses, it is possible to identify the degree to which outcomes are produced by processes facilitated by the procedures of service system, by exogenous factors, and by interactions of the two.

Elements endogenous to the service system (e.g., interim outcomes) also may moderate long-term service outcomes. In human services, the continued delivery of program procedures often is a function of successful initial outcomes. Drug treatment procedures, for instance, typically are maintained only if interim outcomes ("clean" urine test results indicating no drug use) are obtained within the first few weeks of treatment. Undesirable interim outcomes (e.g., "dirty urines") may result in cessation of treatment procedures (and processes).

Interim outcomes can determine the continuation or change of program procedures. To break out of a cycle of negative interim outcomes that cause deterioration or cessation of procedures and their processes, and that then make more negative outcomes likely, new procedures can be added or current procedures can be abandoned. For example, the overly stressed stress management clients may receive medication to reduce their anxiety to the point where they can understand and carry out stress management procedures. The time management client may be contacted by group leaders by phone immediately prior to meetings to enjoin them to attend. In these ways, interim outcomes determine whether procedures and resulting processes are continued, whereas those procedures and processes in turn determine the success of interim outcomes. The determination of interim outcome by procedures, and vice versa, is reciprocal: a form of *reciprocal determinism* first described by Bandura (1978). Bandura applied this concept to understanding relationships between individuals and their environments that are characterized as "self-control," but the same idea works at a macrolevel for the behavior of service systems.

Similar sorts of reciprocal determinism are seen more directly in relationships between processes and outcomes. As one continues in therapy for social anxiety, for instance, one gains additional social skills. As one uses these skills, higher and more positive levels of social interaction are achieved. These interim outcomes increase one's expectations that one can say and do the appropriate thing in social situations to be encountered in the future. These psychological processes (the expectancies in this case) in turn improve frequency of exposure to and learning from social situations, which lead to yet more positive outcomes.

One implication of reciprocal determinism is that outcomes need to be assessed in ways that capture many possible relationships between procedures, processes, and outcomes. This chapter provides basic concepts, distinctions, and strategies for outcome assessment. Entire books are devoted to measuring and evaluating the outcomes of human services with at best a portion of a chapter devoted to the assessment of costs and possibly a chapter devoted to assessment of procedures (e.g., Posavac & Carey, 1989). Here, we can hope to cover only aspects of outcome assessment that are most important in CPPOA and that are not typically covered in evaluation texts.

Tailored Versus Generalizable Definitions of Outcomes

Most methods of assessing outcomes, especially those involving standard instruments, ask the same questions of all clients. This *nomothetic* approach to assessment (Lamiell, 1981; Silverstein, 1988) is common, and has the advantage of yielding data from each client that can be combined with data from other clients so that statistical analyses can be performed. Often, the unique types of outcomes experienced by individual clients are not reflected in nomothetic assessments. For example, one client receiving group therapy may come to enjoy a more satisfying family life and may make new friends, whereas another client in the same group may enjoy significant enhancements in health and in career development. Often, it seems that different clients experience outcomes so diverse that many positive results of treatment go unnoticed when the same circumscribed outcomes are examined for all clients in minute detail.

A purely *idiographic* approach to assessment, which attempts to capture data for a specific individual (Lamiell, 1981; Silverstein, 1988), does not attempt to find a common ground for the outcomes of all clients. Idiographic and related approaches to assessment may maximize detection of improvements in individuals' lives at the expense of measuring outcomes in a manner that allows findings to be generalized to other clients or other service systems. It is possible, however, to begin with a largely idiographic approach to defining the outcomes of treatment and then bring it up to a more general level of measurement.

For example, Siegert and Yates (1980) attempted to integrate idiographic and nomothetic approaches to outcome assessment by asking parents to set as goals the significant reduction or elimination of the three most vexing problems displayed by their children. Parents differed greatly in the problems cited—from playing music too loud to swearing at authority figures. Siegert and Yates summarized the short-term effects of child management training by calculating the percentages of reduction in each of the targeted behaviors between the 2-week baseline period and the end of the 5-week training program. The average of the three percentages was the outcome measure. Subjects evidenced systematic, reasonably consistent reductions in the target behaviors, as shown in Figure 4.1.

Another approach to dealing with both the uniqueness of individual needs in human services and the importance of being able to summarize the results of services across clients is goal attainment scaling (Kiresuk & Lund, 1978). Most variations on this scale allow the client and change agent to work together to determine both the areas of the client's life in which changes will be attempted and what would constitute different degrees of significant positive and negative changes. The result is a highly individualized service plan and outcome assessment system. Table 4.1 shows a goal attainment scale for counseling of a woman recently made homeless by separation from her common-law husband. Goals are reflected in specific

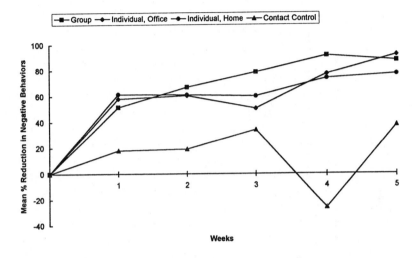

Figure 4.1. Interim Outcomes of Three Alternative Delivery Systems for Child Management Training
SOURCE: Derived from data presented by Siegert and Yates (1980).

entries made in the cells by the counselor and the woman following discussions of what, for her, are desired and reasonable goals.

Yet another way in which individual responses to services can be taken into account in the assessment of outcomes is to use an array of measures so that the particular areas in which a client exhibits improvement (or possibly harm) are more likely to be among those assessed. For example, a mental health clinic might administer measures of anxiety, depression, and social functioning to capture outcomes produced by their services. A residential program for problem children might employ measures of a large set of negative and positive behaviors (Yates et al., 1979) in the hope that change would be registered on some behavioral measures for some clients and other behavioral measures for other clients. Change agents may be in the best position to know which dimensions of functioning are most likely to be improved by the service system.

Yet another way to combine nomothetic and idiographic methods of assessing program outcomes may be to use *adaptive testing* (Embretson,

Table 4.2

Goal Approximation Rating Form, Global Assessment Package (GARF-GAP)

	Most Unfavorable Outcome Likely	Less Than Expected Success	Expected Level of Success	More Than Expected Success	Best Anticipated Success
Housing	No regular shelter	Regular shelter at friend's or relative's house but no private space (e.g., sleeping on a couch)	Lives in rent subsidized one-bedroom apartment with family	Lives in group home sharing room with one adult	Lives in own apartment or cottage
Education	No further education	Begins, but does not complete, GED course	Receives GED	Receives GED and begins but does not complete vocational training program	Receives GED and completes vocational training program
Social relations	Family and old friends continue to ostracize	Resumes regular relationship with one family member or friend	Family gives "second chance," such as invitations to dinner at family matriarch's house	Taken back into family (invited to weddings, funerals); regularly invited to outings, parties by friends	Resumes "key player" role in family; becomes a central member in a group of friends
Employment	Looks for jobs 2 or more days a week, but has no part-time or full-time work	Finds a temporary part-time or full-time job that ends within 1 month	Finds a permanent part-time job with little possibility for advancement	Permanent part-time or full-time job; enrolls in manager training program	Is self-employed and managing others in a commercial business

1992). This method of assessment follows a branching algorithm that determines with a few initial items the areas in which most change has been made. Often, a computer is used to implement the branching rules quickly, drawing on a large bank of possible items. Those areas then are assessed by a similar method, with items selected to determine the level at which a skill or personality characteristic can be tested in as efficient a manner as possible. Regardless of how the testing was done, however, the results still would need to be transformed in a manner that allowed combination of data from the various measures.

Integrating Information From
Multiple Outcome Perspectives

After discussing outcome assessment with many interest groups and following careful consideration of the degree to which it is possible to assess outcomes in ways advocated by interest groups, it may be necessary to combine information from many measures. Differences in the validity of the measures, or in the relevance of an interest group to the key decision maker, may dictate that each measure should not be given equal importance in the bottom line of outcome assessment. This can be accomplished by weighting each outcome measure for its importance, perhaps relative to the other measures, as is suggested by multiattribute utility theory (e.g., Edwards & Newman, 1982) or using metric conjoint analysis (Krantz & Tversky, 1971; Louviere, 1988).

To obtain a single composite measure of outcome for use in cost-effectiveness analysis or CPPOA, measures that are to be disregarded receive a weighting of zero by default; of course, determination of importance weightings requires more effort for measures that are to be included. Decision makers could be surveyed to determine the relative importance of different measures, as was done by Yates et al. (1979). Each measure could be rated on a 5-point or 10-point scale for its relative importance, and ratings could be standardized for different raters. Such surveys can result in importance weights that are greater than one if the measure is judged more important than the average measure and less than one if the measure is judged to be less important than the average measure.

The primary remaining problem in using a combination of outcome measures is making their units similar. It might not be useful, for instance, to evaluate an alcohol abuse mitigation program by simply summing (a) change in a locus of control score between the beginning and end of therapy and (b) change in arrests recorded for drunk driving. Instead, either a common unit needs to be found for these measures or they need to be reported and analyzed separately. Percentage of change in the measures provides one common metric, as noted earlier; percentage of approximation to goals yields another.

STRATEGIES FOR OUTCOME ASSESSMENT

Getting Better: Outcomes as
Improved Biopsychosocial Functioning

The outcomes usually measured by researchers in psychology, sociology, social work, nursing, and related professions are *behaviors* (e.g., attendance at school or work, time spent with children, skill at public speaking), *cognitions* (e.g., suicidal ideation), *emotions* (e.g., feelings of alienation or dissociation), or *biological states* (e.g., immune system functioning). Numerous measures have been developed for these cognitions, emotions, and states. From the perspectives of most funders and decision makers, however, these so-called outcomes really are only the means to more socially significant and observable ends, such as cessation of spouse abuse, keeping out of jail, employment, securing housing, and economic self-sufficiency. When pressed, many human service providers also will acknowledge that changes in emotion, self-realization, or other goal indices are important in their own rights but are not the ultimate outcomes for which services are being funded. Although changes inside the head or body of the client are the goal of most procedures for which psychologists and other change agents receive formal training, the long-term goals of most human services typically are more pragmatic, more economic, more observable—and (conveniently) more readily assessed.

Improvement

Many agents of change—especially those working with clients who are challenged physically, intellectually, or developmentally—hope to help clients maximize their potential. Bringing this around to something operational, however, means talking about some sort of concrete achievement in the areas of relationships with others, employment, education, health, and so on. This is the basic approach of the level of functioning scales proposed by Carter and Newman (1976) and realized in the Global Assessment Scale (GAS; Endicott, Spitzer, Fleiss, & Cohen, 1976), which became Axis V of the *Diagnostic and Statistical Manual of Mental Disorders (DSM)* of the American Psychiatric Association (see also Newman & Sorensen, 1985).

The GAS is a rating scale for psychiatrists to use when assessing the global psychological and social functioning of an individual during the past week. The scale ranges from 1 to 100. Definitions and brief examples of functioning at each 10-point range (e.g., 1-10, 11-20, 91-100) are provided. Raters are asked to select the range that describes the person's lowest functioning in the preceding week: for instance,

> 51-60: Moderate symptoms OR generally functioning with some difficulty (e.g., few friends and flat affect, depressed mood, and pathological self-doubt, euphoric mood and pressure of speech, moderately severe antisocial behavior). (Endicott et al., 1976, p. 768)

A specific number then is selected within the 10-point range (e.g., 54) based on the rater's assessment of where the subject lies within the functioning continuum.

Approximation to Normalcy

Many mental health service systems wish to return clients to so-called normal functioning, as that is defined by the community or the change agents. *Normalcy* can be defined quantitatively as receiving scores, ratings, or behavior counts that are within the normal range. The limits of this range can be defined as what is not significantly different from mean scores on critical variables. For example, what is normal for a high school student in a particular community could be defined according to the modal or median (a) grades, (b) aptitude test scores, (c) dates, (d) hours spent at a part-time job, and (e) other variables deemed critical and common for students in the community. Yates et al. (1979) defined normal as having an average behavior frequency that was within two standard deviations of the average behavior frequency recorded for children who were not receiving residential treatment.

How normal a client is, before or after receiving services, could be quantified by comparing the client's grades, test scores, dates, and hours worked during a representative period of time to the average on the same variables during the same period of time for persons of the same gender and age. Rather than calling a client abnormal if he or she does not exhibit behavior within a statistically acceptable range, the approximation to normalcy could be reflected in the difference between client scores and normal scores, ratings, or frequencies. This difference could be standardized by dividing the difference by the standard deviation of the normal group. A *percentage of normal* measure might be calculated, too. For example, how closely an anorexic client's weight approximated normal weight might be calculated by dividing the client's weight (e.g., 75 pounds) by the normal weight for the client's height, age, and gender (e.g., 100 pounds), resulting in 75% normalcy. Percentage change from pretreatment to posttreatment in normalcy could gauge the contribution made by treatment and other factors.

Ratings of how normal a primary client acts or talks also could be obtained from secondary clients who are in regular contact with the client. These ratings, however, are more likely to be influenced by labels that might have been assigned to the client when she or he was disturbed and that continue to bias others' perception of client actions (Langer & Abelson, 1974; Yates & Hoage, 1982). Also, asking community representatives to define the norm for their community may yield what is considered to be minimally acceptable good behavior rather than what is the statistically normal (i.e., average or modal) behavior.

Approximation to Goals

Whereas helping clients become more normal is the goal of some change agents, helping clients become better than normal is the goal of others. This could be operationalized as maximizing the percentage of approximation of goal levels of functioning, of goal behavior frequencies, of goal ratings, or of targeted levels of proficiency. Most of the same methods used to measure approximation to normalcy can be used to assess approximation to goals, because "normal" is just one of many possible goals. The advantage of selecting statistical normalcy as a goal is that what is normal may be more readily measured and may be less controversial than what is actually desired from particular clients.

Culturally Relative Norms and Goals

It is possible, however, that what is normal for one community may be inappropriate for another community. For example, the people who are included in the sample that defines normal scores, ratings, or frequencies might be principally of one race, religion, or socioeconomic class (e.g., European American, Protestant, and middle-class). This could bias assessments of outcomes to favor the lifestyle of those people. When outcomes on approximation to statistical normalcy were fed back to service providers, procedures might be changed in ways that would encourage clients from minority cultures to abandon their lifestyles and goals and to adopt those of the majority culture. Biased norms also could produce evaluations that favored programs that treated majority rather than minority clients:

The former clients would be more likely to exhibit so-called normal behavior.

Another reason to use goal-oriented rather than norm-oriented outcome assessments is the possibility that what is normal is not desirable. In education, in body weight, and in health, the norm of most populations is not what much of society deems to be desirable. In these instances, clients (tertiary, secondary, and possible primary) can be polled to select goals in a manner that is less arbitrary than allowing a researcher to decide what is right for the client.

It also may be important to set different goals for different types of clients. Erroneous conclusions about differences in outcomes could result from the use of radically different goals, of course. Some cultural groups might claim that other cultural groups had set lower goals and thus had an unfair advantage in comparisons of the effects of human services in their communities. It is likely, for instance, that a suburban upper-middle-class European American community might set "master's-level graduate degree" and "living in a variety of major urban centers" as reasonable and desirable goals for its young adults, whereas a rural European American community might set "finishing high school on time" and "raising a family on the farm" as optimal goals for its young adults.

A possible resolution of this sort of goal conflict is to develop separate goals and goal-related measures for each culture. Although services then would be designed to meet the goals specified by the local culture, the measures developed for each culture could be applied to all clients in a comprehensive evaluation. Concrete definitions of goals might be derived from surveys of the community or of community leaders. For example, what are *really bad* (1), *worse than average* (2), *usual* (3), *better than average* (4), and *really good* (5) levels of functioning in (a) housing, (b) education, (c) social relationships, and (d) employment could be specified by a group composed of a minister, an elected local official, a high school teacher or principal, and a law enforcement officer. A form similar to Table 4.1, which is a subset of a procedure developed by Yates et al. (1993) to measure outcomes of drug treatment other than cessation of substance abuse, could be used to rate client functioning in each sector of the client's life, relative to goals. Eventually, ratings of these five levels of functioning in these four areas could be standardized.

Getting Worse

Getting better and its derivative measures are not the only things to assess. Although there often is understandable reluctance to consider how one's services might produce negative outcomes, there may be real (if transient) side effects of services, such as stigmatization by one's self and others or grief and anger over one's (and others') past behavior. Measuring these may be necessary to allay concerns on the part of some interest groups regarding possible side effects of treatment and also to provide a ready response to critics. In addition, by including negative outcomes in CPPOA it may be possible to understand what service procedures and processes have led to the undesirable outcomes so these can be minimized. Finally, CPPOA may be able to contrast (e.g., via path analyses) the degree to which negative outcomes are attributable to exogenous factors (e.g., age, death of a child, loss of employment due to liquidation of one's employer) rather than to the services provided.

Prevention: Outcomes as
Dysfunction Averted or Postponed

Reducing the risk of health problems, of unemployment, and of negative events in general seems to be the goal of many human services. Although actual behaviors are all that can be measured directly in outcome assessment, research occasionally provides solid predictions of what is likely to occur in the future as a result of current practices. For areas of human activity in which these predictions have been shown to be valid (e.g., smoking and future risk of heart disease, lung disease, and cancer; unsafe sexual practices and STDs), outcomes can be measured as risks averted or reduced. It even seems possible to predict the occurrence or continuation of risky behaviors (e.g., continued smoking, continued unprotected anal receptive sex) from prior behavior and from cognitive processes, such as expectancies (e.g., Aspinwall, Kemeny, Taylor, Schneider, & Dudley, 1991; Chassin, Presson, Sherman, & Edwards, 1991). This approach may be especially useful for programs that attempt to prevent with early (e.g., childhood) interventions high-cost but common problems, such as heart disease, cancer, substance abuse, unemployment, and criminal lifestyles. Essentially, use of validated predictors of long-term outcomes amounts to measuring interim outcomes, or even processes, that have been shown to be economical or more timely surrogates for measures of long-term outcomes. In this practice, there is, of course, the risk of assuming that predictions are completely accurate. Outcome assessments based on one or more predictive associations between long-term and interim outcome, or between interim outcome and processes modified by treatment, are only as valid as the weakest predictive link.

"Real" Benefits: Outcomes as
Income Increments or Profits Produced

Interest groups that are not as active in the community or as interested in client welfare may dictate definitions and measures of desirable outcomes that cannot be measured via the strategies described earlier. In particular, parties that fund many human services are interested in both the welfare of the individual and the extent to which that individual contributes to, or is a burden on, society. One way to measure so-called contributions to society is to find out if society pays out more than it gets back from the individual, such as the difference between the amount of support (e.g., welfare payments) that society provides to the individual and the income generated by that individual. This difference can, of course, be expected to vary over the lifetime of the individual. Societal investment probably exceeds income and other contributions for the first two decades of life, for many persons, followed by a period of an increasingly positive "balance of payments" between society and the individual, with a return to more support than contribution in the middle and later years of life. In addition to showing the net contribution (or support) for individuals receiving services, it may be useful to compare the client's net contribution to the net contribution of persons of the same age in the same society or culture. Comparisons of the change in net contribution before versus during and after a program could be especially powerful. Some contributions to society, such as creative works, are more difficult to quantify.

Gross and net income are potential measures of outcome for human services. Many third parties, particularly taxpayers and employers, treat outcome measures that have monetary units as being intrinsically valid, even though measures such as *future dollars saved* may be as low in reliability and validity as measures that do not come in dollar units. Still, the high importance assigned to monetary measures of outcome by what are critical interest groups in many evaluations often requires that these measures be considered. An additional reason to consider monetary measures of outcome is that this usually is required for a cost-benefit analysis to be performed. As noted in the first chapter, cost-benefit analysis requires that both costs and benefits be measured in the same units; if resources consumed by a service system are measured in monetary units, then so must outcomes.

Just as there are a variety of strategies for assessing outcomes in terms of improved behavioral, cognitive, emotional, or biological functioning, so are there several ways to assess the economic well-being and functioning of a client. If a client is employed or has returned to employment as a result of a job placement or rehabilitation program, the income and benefits received by that client are direct measures of actual income benefits

(Silkman, Kelley, & Wolf, 1983; Yates, 1985). Increased earnings in a company that instituted an Employee Assistance Program would be another actual benefit to be assessed (Fiedler & Wight, 1989; Jones & Vischi, 1979). Paycheck stubs, any benefits paid by employers, and the value of perquisites all provide information about the economic status of employed individuals. Payroll computer files are possible sources for this information, as are income tax records. Net income (gross income minus expenses) can be used to monitor the economic well-being of self-employed persons. Self-reports of these monetary data may be superior, if they are anonymous, to income tax reports, although the latter offer a standardized format for accessing the necessary information (Calsyn et al., 1993). Self-report of employment income, in particular, seems to be reliable over multiyear periods (Anglin, Hser, & Chou, 1993). Accounting records may need careful inspection to avoid overestimating positive outcomes due to special practices sometimes used to record transactions, liabilities, and assets. Computer files and databases are likely to be available for individual and corporate income data and can be edited to exclude information not needed by the assessor.

Naturally, assessing outcomes in monetary units does not preclude the use of other, nonmonetary measures of outcome. In fact, evaluations can begin with measures that are most appropriate to program outcomes and can then monetize the outcomes found. In this way, the superior reliability of many measures of nonmonetary program outcomes is largely preserved when estimating monetary program outcomes. Predictions of future earnings, for example, can be derived by assuming that training clients in a particular skill will, with a certain probability, qualify them for careers in a particular profession. One can then assume that they will earn the average salary in that profession as opposed to the average salaries in their previous occupations—the difference in salaries being a measure of the monetary outcome of the program. This salary increment then would be summed for the expected time each individual would remain in the profession (and, of course, present-valued as described in the chapter on cost assessment). Predictions such as these should, however, take into account the range of salaries possible in different occupations and the probability that many occupations will change dramatically or be eliminated in the coming decades.

Cost-Savings Benefits:
Outcomes as Resource Expenditures Saved

Concepts

The same perspectives that may define outcomes according to net monetary gain by the person, community, or corporation also may consider the avoidance of expected monetary outlays as positive. With varying degrees of predictability, funds are spent by government agencies, companies, and individuals in response to problems that could have been solved by certain human services. To the extent that a service can solve or prevent the problem, it can reduce or eliminate these expenditures. Stress management training, for example, might be shown to save health care expenses related to stress and to reduce outlays for part-time employees who had to substitute for full-time workers taking sick leave due to stress (Manuso, 1978). The saved funds are then freed for other social or financial investments. This sort of cost savings benefit is different from the profit sort of benefit described earlier but is especially important to assess for human services.

For service systems that work with families, communities, or companies as their client, measures of cost-savings benefits can include the economic well-being of the family or economic indicators of community prosperity (e.g., median per capita income for the locale). These services may produce increments in earnings that are substantial, especially when the predicted cumulative effects of the service on lifetime earnings are contrasted with the lifetime earnings without the service. Yates (1986b), for example, estimated that in the United States, the lifetime income lost to suicides committed in 1983 was $6.54 billion, a portion of which could be claimed as a cost-savings benefit by suicide prevention programs that had valid data on their effectiveness.

The extent to which the individual is less of a burden on society (i.e., requiring a smaller amount of resources from society) as a result of receiving a service also can be a measure of a desirable outcome of that service. For instance, funders often hope that one outcome of substance abuse programs is reduced criminal behavior by clients. The observed, self-reported, or estimated reduction in each type of crime can be multiplied by the cost of crimes performed by addicts to estimate the savings attributable to a drug treatment program (e.g., Harwood, Hubbard, Collins, & Rachal, 1988).

Reductions in other nonmonetary measures of outcome can be converted into estimated cost-savings benefits. For example, treatment for schizophrenia provided in a transitional lodge environment can reduce the cost of treatment from approximately $25 per patient per day for traditional inpatient care to approximately $5 per patient per day in a transitional lodge (Fairweather, Sanders, Maynard, & Cressler, 1969). After treatment, 30% to 70% of lodge patients were employed full-time during the 40 months following discharge, paying taxes and contributing to the economy, whereas less than 5% of traditionally treated patients were employed full-time

(Fairweather et al., 1969). The difference in welfare payments required for 95% of the traditionally treated patients versus 70% (or fewer) of the lodge patients would be another cost-savings benefit to estimate and report. Truly successful treatment also might be expected to save the costs of additional treatment. It is tempting to take figures for the cost of treatment and add them to the cost-savings benefits as well, adjusting them for the probability that a client might return for treatment in the future. Returning for booster sessions and discerning the need to commit oneself to additional treatment may well be laudable outcomes that will result in better long-term outcomes. This seeking of additional treatment in the future, however, also should produce a greater net cost-savings benefit in the long run. Certainly, a treatment that keeps clients out of trouble and out of future treatment would have larger cost-savings benefits than a treatment that kept clients out of trouble but encouraged them to seek additional treatment. For example, Fairweather et al. (1969) found that in addition to the previously mentioned cost savings of about $20 per patient per day (in 1965 dollars) in treatment expenses, discharged lodge patients spent 80% to 100% of a 40-month follow-up period outside the hospital (presumably consuming less expensive outpatient services, if any), whereas comparison patients spent only 20% to 30% of the same follow-up period outside the hospital. Substantial cost savings also have been found when adding psychological services to medical treatment (e.g., Cummings, Pallak, Dorken, & Henke, 1992; Pallak, Cummings, Dorken, & Henke, 1994). Careful monitoring of other outcomes and unmet needs of other services would be a good idea, of course, in evaluations claiming reduced use of services as a cost-savings benefit.

Strategies for Assessing Cost-Savings Benefits: Avoiding Overestimation (and Underestimation)

Cost-savings benefits can be measured in several ways. An ideal method begins by assigning clients from a large, homogeneous pool to a control group or to one of several alternative human service mixes. Expenditures made by agencies for each group of clients and spending by each group of clients then is assessed prior to, during, and following the delivery of human services. Often, it is the cost of future services that is saved by the provision of services early in the development of the problem (or before the problem begins to develop). The difference in mean expenditures during and following services can be tested for statistical significance and is the cost-savings benefit. Cost-savings may occur for several years following a service. If the effect of a service can be measured over the lifetime of an individual, such as reduced risk of heart disease through life following a smoking cessation program for heart attack victims, cost-savings benefits can be compiled over the same period. More concretely, here is one four-step way to estimate cost-savings benefits:

1. Measure the reduction in mental health, health, and other problems that occurs as a result of the program being evaluated (this should involve the use of experimental design, such as random assignment to a treatment and waiting-list control group).

2. Estimate what the costs of those problems would have been to the individuals without the program (this estimate can be derived from study of the continuation of the problem in the waiting-list control group).

3. Estimate the costs attributable to the same problems that are likely to occur to the same individuals because the program is not 100% effective in eliminating the problem and in preventing reoccurrence of the problem.

4. Estimate any costs that would result from the program (e.g., seeking additional medical or educational services due to increased understanding of one's problem, or seeking services to deal with unanticipated negative side effects of the program).

A set time period must be decided on for outcome and cost-savings assessment: 5 to 10 years is a common period, although lifetimes offer a more socially meaningful period over which to assess outcomes and cost. It may be most accurate to express outcomes and costs in a probabilistic manner. For example, cost types mentioned in Step 3 might be calculated as (the probability of the problem recurring in the future period) × (the probability of receiving human services for the recurring problem during the period) × (the cost of the future services that would be used in attempts to solve the recurring problem).

To reflect the size of the future period and its effect on the delayed cost of services, we would have to use the present value of the cost figure resulting from this calculation (calculated as detailed in the cost assessment chapter). To avoid overestimation of the value of delayed savings, Yates (1986b) considered the present value of the estimated lifetime earnings lost to suicide of $6.54 billion (after adjusting for other sources of mortality). The result was a marked reduction to $2.97 billion in lifetime earnings lost.

To be comprehensive, these cost calculations would have to be performed for each psychological, social, educational, criminal, and health problem that might occur in the future at lower rates in clients who received the service in question. The cost savings potentially produced by the human service would be the difference between the sums of future service costs for persons who did receive the service being evaluated and those who did not. There is much room for uncertainty and exaggeration (and underestimation) here, so the methods of cost savings assessment need to be rigorous. Generally, it is better to be conservative in estimating cost savings and other forms of benefit because one then can argue that, if anything, the benefits actually will be higher than estimated. This counterbalances the rather natural tendency to underestimate costs and overestimate benefits.

A basic strategy for dealing with this uncertainty is to report separate cost savings values for (a) largest probable, (b) smallest probable, and (c) most likely projections (Yates, 1980c, 1980d). For some services (such as preschool education or smoking cessation), the differences in expenditures (such as remedial education or heart operations) may not occur between the served and nonserved groups until years or decades following service delivery. To capture this sort of "sleeper benefit," the ability to accurately predict expenditures for health, mental health, and other services decades in the future is crucial. Research may be able to document the predictive power of interim outcomes and even of client processes, as suggested earlier. Without empirical support, however, estimation of future cost-savings benefits is an informed guess at best and more often, a misleading figure that overestimates or underestimates the resources eventually consumed because a service was offered or withheld many years earlier.

Estimation of cost-savings benefits also can be exaggerated by assuming that if the mental health, health, or other problem is removed or prevented, clients will not experience the problem again. For example, when estimating the benefits of suicide prevention, it is necessary to recognize that even when suicide is prevented, some clients, in all age ranges, will die due to other causes. It is tempting, but a possible exaggeration, to say that for each suicide prevented, one has saved the lifetime earnings of that person. If one starts out with a group of 10,000,000 clients of which 100 would be expected to commit suicide during a 5-year period, and if one assumes that none of the 100 would have committed suicide following participation in the prevention program, it remains probable that some of those 100 clients would die during the same 5 years due to other causes (e.g., accidents, cancer, heart disease). When assessing cost-savings benefits, it is important to not assume that one has cured all the potential problems the client will face in the coming years. Quantitatively, this requires one to subtract from the number of work years saved by the suicide prevention program the proportion of clients who would be expected to die due to other factors during the period over which suicide was prevented.

Estimation of cost-savings benefits also may be excessive if the analysis assumes that when the problem is not removed or prevented by formal treatment, it would not disappear, diminish, or be prevented by other, natural processes. Of course, a number of health and mental health problems do have rates of spontaneous remission that are greater than zero. This source of error can be addressed by measuring the cost-savings benefits experienced by comparison groups that received a diminished form (or none) of the service.

SELECTING INSTRUMENTS FOR OUTCOME ASSESSMENT

Parameters of Outcome Assessment

Many of the concepts introduced for the assessment of resources, procedures, and processes also work for the measurement of outcomes. For instance, just as different interest groups (e.g., clients, agents of change, researchers) may have different perspectives on costs, so may they view outcomes differently (as has already been noted for monetary outcomes). Interest group perspectives may interact with levels of specificity and temporal considerations such that primary clients are interested in more specific and immediate outcomes (e.g., fewer negative behaviors from children, not having to buy drugs) whereas tertiary clients may be interested in more general and delayed outcomes (e.g., reduced expenditures for social services in the future, reduced taxes, less crime, higher company profit). Secondary clients, such as spouses, may wish for reduced physical abuse and increased income. Researchers may hope for change on theoretically important measures in the predicted direction and at acceptable levels of statistical significance. Each perspective deserves consideration in assessments of the outcomes of social services, which usually results in multiple measures of outcome.

Finding Measures

Usually, one measure of outcome does not work for all interest groups for all human services. The concept of *level of functioning* (e.g., Carter & Newman, 1976; Newman & Sorensen, 1985) is perhaps the broadest, most portable, and most acceptable approach to outcome assessment, but it may lack the specificity needed to show differences expected by some interested parties between certain procedures or programs. In discrete areas of human services, a small set of outcome assessment instruments may become the standard accepted by most researchers and clinicians. These measures often can be discerned by searching the research literature on either the treatment procedures (e.g., short-term analytic therapy) or outcomes of interest (e.g., adjustment to learning that one is HIV-positive). Consensus conferences devoted to the procedures or outcomes of interest also may reveal the most important and useful measures of outcomes. If so, outcome assessment may be relatively simple.

It is more likely, however, that several measures will be vying for a position as *the* measure in the field. This may be revealed by consultation with experts or via literature searches (e.g., using PsycINFO's PsychLIT© CD-ROM database or related versions accessible through computer networks such as BRS's After Dark® or CompuServe's IQuest). The safest way to proceed, then, is to administer the measures most likely to succeed. In the area of substance abuse, for example, the Addiction Severity Index (McLellan, Luborsky, Cacciola, Griffith, Evans, et al., 1985; McLellan, Luborsky, Cacciola, Griffith, McGahan, et al., 1985; McLellan, Luborsky, Woody, & O'Brien, 1980) has been a principal measure for over a decade and a half, but the Individual Assessment Profile (Flynn et al., 1992) has gained recognition as a questionnaire that includes measures of critical procedures and processes as well as measures of outcome. Other measures used in substance abuse treatment contexts, such as drug courts, include the Substance Abuse Subtle Screening Inventory (Miller, 1988).

Many texts provide additional strategies for assessing outcomes that range from recording behavior frequencies to obtaining ratings of client achievement on the sort of goal attainment scales described earlier (Cronbach, 1982; Kazdin, 1992). What is critical for any measure of outcome is to make sure that it has the basic qualities and abilities that are necessary for any form of measurement. Without these basic qualities, it is difficult to reach conclusions about the outcomes of a service and about relationships between outcomes and processes, procedures, and costs. The measurement qualities of reliability and validity are detailed in Campbell and Stanley (1963) and elsewhere (e.g., Anastasi, 1976; Kazdin, 1992); they are reviewed here briefly. These same characteristics of good measures are necessary for processes, procedures, and resources, naturally, as well as for outcomes. Often, reviews of measures will discuss and include indices of the following qualities.

A good measure is like a ruler. The measure should not change when it is brought from one environment to another or from one time to another. Like a ruler, the measure should generate the same readings no matter who uses it so long as the users have received adequate training in its use and interpretation. The measure should be, in a word, reliable. Like a ruler, the measure should be meaningful in that it is related in predictable ways to other measures. And as a given ruler will have certain predictable relationships to other types of rulers (e.g., English to metric) and to inches-to-miles scales shown on blueprints and maps, so a measure of outcome should be related to other measures that may differ in expense, objectivity, and comprehensiveness. Self-reports of drug use, for example, should be related to urine and hair tests for consumption and byproducts of those drugs. A good outcome measure should, in a word, have high validity.

Reliabilities

There are several types of reliability to consider in measurement. Briefly, a measure of outcome should yield some category or number that is the same over time for individuals who, according to other indicators, should not have changed. This *temporal* or *test-retest reliability* should be high over periods of weeks and months, although reliability generally declines over longer periods. *Interjudge reliability* (sometimes called *interrater reliability*) shows that different persons who have received similar training in the use of the measure arrive at similar conclusions (e.g., generate similar scores) when applying the measure to the same person. If a measure has several parts that are supposed to assess the same thing (such as several items that are designed to measure the stability of one's self-image), the data generated by each part should be similar (the responses to each item, for instance, should be about the same). This is *interitem reliability.* Some instruments are available in several different forms to avoid the possible effects of completing the same instrument repeatedly. (A client might, for example, feel he or she should respond to the same items in the same way as last month, even though substantial changes had occurred that warranted different responses.) The (hoped for) similarity of client responses to different forms of an instrument is called *alternative form reliability.*

Validities

Whereas these types of reliability reflect how well the measurement instrument hangs together, validity judges what the instrument is good for. Returning to the ruler analogy, a ruler that shows inches is useful only if most maps, charts, and tools are in units that are related to inches. The relationship between one measure of outcome and other indicators rarely is as direct, however, as the relationship between one ruler and another or between a ruler and the scale (e.g., inches to miles) on a road map. Many measures of outcome are economical stand-ins for more expensive measures. Most questionnaires, for example, ask questions of clients that are similar to those that an expert interviewer might ask. The findings of most measures are compared to the findings of expert persons or other measures that already have proven themselves to be expert. The degree to which an instrument agrees with experts or previously accepted assessment devices is its *criterion validity* (the expert or accepted instrument is the criterion).

Often, measures of outcome are taken while the client still is receiving the service or has just completed participation in the program. Many times, unfortunately, procedures followed in the service are designed to attain not the intermediate outcomes assessed by the instrument but outcomes that are considerably more significant but also more delayed, as noted earlier. For example, a program for AIDS risk reduction could be evaluated according to a questionnaire measuring knowledge about routes of HIV transmission and the risks imposed by various sexual and intravenous drug use behaviors. The questionnaire might be given immediately following an AIDS education workshop. The outcomes of real interest, however, may be infection by HIV, transmission of HIV, and development of AIDS. The HIV knowledge questionnaire may be the outcome measure used in an evaluation of an AIDS risk reduction program, but it is only a surrogate measure and (it is hoped) a predictor of HIV acquisition. The degree to which such a questionnaire might predict development of AIDS in subsequent years would reflect the predictive validity of the HIV knowledge measure.

The predictive validity of measures is relative. For example, the predictive validity of an HIV knowledge questionnaire could be compared to the degree to which client reports of actual HIV transmission behaviors predicted AIDS. Studies might show that self-reports of transmission behaviors following AIDS awareness groups were better predictors of AIDS several years later. In this case, only instruments with the highest predictive validity would be used in service evaluation.

Other types of validity include *content* (or *face*) *validity, discriminant validity, incremental validity,* and *construct validity.* The degree to which a measure seems, on the face of it, to be measuring what it is supposed to measure is its content validity. Items that refer to marital bliss (e.g., "How often do you find yourself staring at your spouse with a silly smile spread all across your face?") or marital problems (e.g., "How often do you think about leaving your spouse forever?") would give a marriage harmony survey a reasonable amount of content validity. It is possible for an instrument to have low content validity but to register high on predictive and other forms of validity.

A measure that distinguishes between different types of clients (e.g., those who do and do not have substantial marital difficulties) has some amount of discriminative validity. The clearer the distinction and the greater the ability to draw fine distinctions accurately, the greater the discriminative validity. When a new instrument offers greater predictive power or other advantages over standard or previously used instruments, the new instrument is said to have incremental validity. Only when a series of studies demonstrates predicted relationships between a new measure and other, accepted measures does the new measure achieve a degree of construct validity.

Testing outcome instruments for each of the types of reliability and validity is time-consuming and may cause major delays in assessment of outcomes. Some researchers proceed only after content validity has been established. If they find differences between certain groups of clients (e.g., those who received a particular service versus those who did not), validity is declared to be high. If no difference is found, the measure often is blamed. In fact, in all instances, one simply does not know whether the measure yielded an erroneous difference or lack of difference or whether the difference was not in fact produced. Correlational analyses of relationships between measures are even more suspect if basic forms of reliability and validity have not been established prior to the evaluation. For these reasons, evaluations that use standard measures often are taken more seriously by professional researchers than are evaluations that use only homegrown instruments. If new measures of unknown reliability and validity are to be used in an outcome assessment, inclusion of standard instruments whose reliability and validity is known (and is high) can ensure that some conclusions can be reached. By using the standard and new measures, at least with a portion of clients, it also may be possible to assess the validity of the new instruments by comparing the findings they generate to findings yielded by the standard measures.

BIAS IN MONETARY
OUTCOME ASSESSMENTS?

It seems likely that many measures, whether of outcome, cost, procedure, or process, are biased against some groups to greater or lesser degrees (McDowell, 1992). Substantial bias in assessment can lead to findings that favor one group more than another (Angoff, 1988). When monetary units are used to describe outcomes, differences of age, gender, and race reflected in typical rates of pay, the likelihood of developing problems that require human services, and duration of life can bias outcome measures (Davis, 1992). Furthermore, when outcome measures show a greater monetary benefit in offering services to one race, gender, or age group more than others, the result may further prejudices that might have caused the differences in the first place.

For example, the lifetime income lost due to suicide (and hence the potential cost-savings with suicide prevention) is inevitably, and considerably, higher for younger than for older individuals: $219.6 million (present-valued) for persons 15 to 19 years of age at the time of suicide versus $37.3 million (present-valued) for people 60 to 64 years of age at the time of suicide (Yates, 1986b). The higher cost of suicide for younger age groups would be expected to cause higher benefit estimates for suicide prevention programs that target (or are most effective for) younger individuals (Bluementhal, 1988; Hayes & Rowan, 1988; Robins, Murphy, & Wilkinson, 1959). Similar findings could be generated for the costs of suicide, and the cost-savings benefit of suicide prevention, for women versus men, and for different ethnic groups. Does this mean that suicide prevention services should target primarily the young, the male, and the ethnic group that earns the most? Some interest groups will assert that the value of life is different from the value of lifetime earnings. Similarly, quantitatively justified discrimination in the provision of services may be ruled by significant interest groups as discrimination nonetheless. One solution to this problem of biased benefit measures is to assign the same cost-savings value to the lives of persons of all ages, each gender, and all ethnic groups.

Clearly, this is not an easy issue. Assessment of outcomes, and all the rest, can be so challenging that one may lose sight of the original purpose of the evaluation: to analyze relationships between costs, procedures, processes, and outcomes so they can be not only understood but improved. This is the topic of the final chapter.

5

Describing and Improving Cost → *Procedure* → *Process* → *Outcome Relationships*

This book began by describing the CPPOA model of cost-outcome analysis and proceeded to focus on strategies for measuring each component of the model—resources, procedures, processes, and outcomes. This chapter explains how relationships between these components can be analyzed, understood, and possibly improved in a systematic manner so that outcomes are enhanced, costs are reduced, or both.

COST → OUTCOME RELATIONSHIPS

Ratios and Differences

Cost-Effectiveness Ratios

The first thing that most people think of when asked to measure cost-effectiveness is to obtain data on outcomes and costs and to divide one by the other. This has been going on for a long time in health and human services (Goldberg, 1991). Costs can be divided by a standard unit of outcome, such as $200 per client whose depression declined below a predetermined threshold for significant clinical depression. Note that the "cost per . . . " figure is different from the simple cost of the procedure. Also, outcomes can be divided by a standard unit of cost, such as 1.23 months of abstinence per $1,000 invested in drug treatment. The number of months of abstinence produced by a resource expenditure of $1,000 tells us much more than just how much it cost to provide the service. Information on the outcome of the service is included in the index, too. If one doesn't remember that the index includes outcome information, or if the nature of the index is not made clear, confusion can result.

For instance, it might cost $100 to provide basic counseling for a depressed client but, because only one of every two clients in the study became significantly less depressed, the cost per *successfully served* client would be double the cost per *served* client. To make more possible an improvement in treatment, cost-outcome ratios might be formed separately for each component of the treatment program. Separate cost-outcome ratios for clients with different backgrounds or histories of illness or treatment also might be a good idea. If it turned out that clients who had lower (i.e., better) cost-outcome ratios had similar backgrounds, illness histories, or prior treatment experiences, improvement efforts might be more reasoned and efficient.

The act of division that forms the cost-to-effectiveness or effectiveness-to-cost ratio reduces the amount of information on costs and outcomes—a mixed blessing. It is easier to remember one number (e.g., $12.50 per pound lost, $15,000 per life saved), although the different units still need to be recalled. There also is a strong temptation to compare cost-effectiveness ratios to decide which procedure or program to continue and which to terminate. For example, suppose Program A's cost-effectiveness is $2,000 per client receiving effective treatment. Also suppose that Program B's cost-effectiveness is $1,600 per effectively treated client. According to these ratios, Program B should be continued and Program A stopped, right? Maybe; maybe not.

For one thing, each program might be treating different clients. Program A's clients may need more services to attain the same improvement in functioning. Or, Program A may operate in a region that required more money for space and personnel, possibly because less was donated. Even if clients and local costs are identical, however, there could be several other reasons to not drop Program A. It might even turn out that Program B should be discontinued, not Program A. By providing information only on the relative value of costs to outcomes, the cost-to-effectiveness ratio tells nothing about the amount of cost and the size of the program. Perhaps Program B is very large, with a budget of $4,000,000 for serving 5,000 clients per year, half (2,500) of whom improve 10 or more points on the Level of Functioning (LOF) Scale ($4,000,000 ÷ 5,000 clients = $800 per client; $800 per client × 50% improving 10 or more LOF points = $1,600 per successfully served client). In contrast, Program A might be very small, with a budget of only $50,000 for 100 clients per year, half (50) of whom also improve 10 points or more on the same LOF scale ($50,000 ÷ 50 clients = $1,000 per client and $2,000 per successfully treated client).

Programs A and B obviously operate on radically different scales. If large-scale programs were no longer tenable due to public concerns about large institutions, Program B would have to be stopped. This might be necessary if draconian funding cuts made a $4,000,000 budget indefensible. Small programs also might be preferred to larger programs by a shift in policy toward community-based programs more attuned to the ethnic or religious background of local residents.

In response to budget cuts, Program B could reduce its budget by cutting staff and renting out some of its space. It is likely, however, that the higher overhead cost of Program B is not completely variable over the relatively brief period of time allowed in most budget adjustments and that its cost per client would rise. Even if Program B delivered treatment of the same effectiveness after downsizing, the cost per effectively treated client could rise if overhead costs were not extremely flexible. It also is possible that the cost-effectiveness function for Program A would allow for a reduction in cost per client at modest increments in budget, making it even more cost-effective. The result would be that, once the absolute level of funding for the programs (i.e., size of program budget) was taken into account, the relationship between cost and outcome might be the same for Programs A and B, or Program A might even be more cost-effective than Program B.

Cost-Benefit Ratios

Ratios of costs to benefits have been used to evaluate numerous health and human service programs (e.g., Harwood et al., 1988; Lewis, Johnson, Chen, & Erickson, 1992). They have all the virtues and limitations noted earlier for ratios of costs to effectiveness, with one possible advantage. Because benefits are outcomes that have been expressed in the same units as costs, the ratio of costs to benefits suggests a ratio of investment to yield. The benefit-to-cost ratio seems to promise that the profitability of a social enterprise can be evaluated by simply inspecting the benefit-to-cost ratio: If it exceeds 1.00 (i.e., if benefits are more than costs), then it appears to be profitable and OK to fund. For example, if a children's car seat program reduces medical expenditures and insurance costs by more dollars than were used by the program, benefits are greater than costs, and benefits divided by costs would exceed 1.00. Social programs can have benefit-to-cost ratios that clearly exceed 1.00. The Perry Preschool Project to prevent delinquency, for example, was found to have a benefit-to-cost ratio of 7.16 when clients were followed until they were 27 years of age (Schweinhart, Barnes, & Weikart, 1993). It seems obvious, at first glance, that such a program pays for itself and thus should be funded.

One gradually realizes, however, that many health and mental health programs can be shown to save or produce (or save *and* produce) more resources than they consume. The problem is that there are limits—severe limits, usually—on the total resources available to fund these services.

Available funding may be much less than the total cost of all programs that have benefit-to-cost ratios exceeding 1.00. Also, funders may share the same long-term (e.g., 10-year) time perspective that was adopted for measurement of benefits. What may matter more to the decision maker is the immediate expenditure of extremely limited funds. Typically, only the most cost-beneficial programs stand a chance of being funded by persons who must demonstrate clear benefits to voters in the 1 to 3 years preceding the next election campaign.

Thus, cost-benefit ratios are not inherently superior to cost-effectiveness ratios. Nevertheless, the relative profitability of human services is exciting to consider. It can be useful to add up the many monetary outcomes of a program. One sees in this sum an accumulation of outcomes with a dollar sign that is simply more impressive to policy makers and funders than is a complex table of diverse measures of program effectiveness. (It is possible to present the table of effectiveness measures, of course, and then to convert each measure of effectiveness to a monetary measure, or benefits. This gives consumers of the evaluation the best of all possible worlds of information: the details, the real measures, and a monetary bottom line.)

The time that elapses before the monetary benefits exceed costs needs to be expressed as well, of course. This information can be built into the cost-benefit ratio, to some degree, by figuring the present value of benefits prior to dividing benefits by cost. Costs may be present-valued as well prior to calculation of the ratio, although benefits often experience more reduction as a result of present-valuing than do costs (because monetary benefits usually occur after resources are spent for human services).

Cost-Benefit Differences

The difference between benefits and costs may be useful to calculate as well. If costs are similar for several programs, the simple difference may be enough to aid comparisons of the programs. Also, program managers may find the net profit of a program (benefits minus costs) useful to know. For example, Yates, Yokley, and Thomas (1994) examined the net benefits of different incentive systems for motivating therapists to see more clients. The benefit was the money that a clinic did not have to pay therapists from outside the program to see clients that the clinic was obligated to treat. Costs included the expense of implementing the plan and the money paid as incentives. Net benefits ranged from –$6,438 per month (the negative sign of this net benefit indicates that costs exceeded benefits) to +$2,636 per month.

Finding the net benefit of a program often is more complex than just adding up the benefits and subtracting the costs from the benefits. The costs of a suicide prevention program, for instance, may occur over a relatively brief period (e.g., 3 months to 1 year), whereas treatment benefits may be hoped to accrue over several decades or even a lifetime. When dealing with long time periods, present valuing needs to be used to avoid exaggeration of delayed benefits. When such vastly different time periods are involved, the effects of present valuing naturally will be seen more for benefits than for costs.

Also, the results of quoting a few dollar figures can be more powerful than they are representative of the actual cost → outcome relationship. Costs for criminal justice procedures appear to have been reduced by $95,000 by a delinquency prevention program in Syracuse, New York, for instance (Lally, Mangione, & Honig, 1988). The different costs were incurred in adjudication of only 4 youths who had participated in the program versus only 12 youths in a control group. These numbers of 4 and 12 are, of course, quite small and may represent chance variations in the background of individuals and their response to treatment. Unfortunately, once the net cost-benefit figure has been uttered, statistical considerations and concerns about generalizability of findings usually melt away before an intensive focus on data with a dollar sign preceding it.

Payback Period

Another way to examine the absolute and relative profitability of a service program is to compute how long it will take for the program to pay back the investment made in resources. This sort of cost-benefit analysis is easiest if the program is of fixed and relatively short duration and if the benefits add up at a measurable rate. For instance, a 3-day corporate creativity enhancement retreat with follow-up sessions at 1, 3, and 6 months includes the definite, finite cost of payments made to creativity enhancement consultants. There also is the somewhat less discernible but real opportunity cost of not having employees working on specific projects during the main and booster sessions. The payback question is how many months or years do we have to wait until the investment in creativity enhancement results in better products, services, or ideas that, in turn, result in better income? Of course, the cost-benefit analysis rarely stops here. Close on the heels of "How long until it pays for itself?" are "Did you adjust for present value?" (if the payback period is over a year) and "Could we have had a quicker or better payback on an alternative investment of our in-service training funds and our employees' time?"

The Oxford House program of self-help and self-housing for former abusers of alcohol and other drugs provides another example of how payback periods could be used to describe cost → benefit relationships (Molloy, 1992). Oxford Houses do not cost much to establish and they may well help former users stay sober and straight. Loans from a $100,000 revolving fund established for each state by Congress are used to secure leases. Say that the revolving fund costs $1,000 to administer annually. Assistance in starting up a house runs about $9,000 per house. Demographics of Oxford House residents suggest that, without involvement in a program, they probably would relapse into severe drug abuse within the first year. The result would be no real income for the state and considerable public expenses for justice, health, and social services to the relapsed abuser.

If the result of the Oxford House program is maintaining drug-free residents, as seems to be the case (Molloy, 1992), then the benefits in taxes paid and public services *not* used might be conservatively estimated as $60,000 annually for a house of 6 individuals. Thus, for a $10,000 investment in the first year, there would be a yield of $60,000 in the first year. The payback period for the investment, or cost, would be approximately 2 months, if one assumes that the $60,000 accrues evenly over months at the rate of $5,000 per month for 12 months. If Oxford House residents used some social services in the first few months, then the payback period still would not exceed the first 6 months: a dramatic return on investment of service dollars that would repay itself manyfold over the lifetimes of house residents.

Where's the Control Group in Cost-Benefit Analysis?

Comparison groups can add important information for all methods of contrasting the benefits of a program to its costs (Weisbrod, 1983). It is difficult to assume, for example, that the income received by clients after special job training is a clear measure of the benefit of the training. It is conceivable, at least to critics of the job training, that some income might have been received if the training was not provided. Unless this possibility can be definitely eliminated, the income that would have occurred without training should be subtracted from the income received by persons with training.

One measure of this "income without training" could be the income received by the same persons prior to training. Changes in employment possibilities, and the effects on employers of simply knowing that a person received special job training, might boost income, however, regardless of or in addition to the actual value of the training. A better measure might be the income received by a very similar group of persons who did not receive job training. Of course, truly comparable groups of persons may be found

Table 5.1

Fishman-Style Cost-Outcome Analysis of Treatment Programs A and B

		Outcomes		
		A > B	A = B	A < B
Costs	A > B	?	B	B
	A = B	A	?	B
	A < B	A	A	?

NOTE: A > B means that outcomes of Program A were found to be better than outcomes of Program B and costs of Program A exceeded costs of Program B. A < B means that outcomes of Program A were found to be inferior to the outcomes of Program B and costs of Program A were less than the costs of Program B.

only by assigning individuals randomly to training and nontraining conditions. Because this has proven difficult in many human services, different methods of examining cost → procedure → process → outcome relationships have been developed. Each has certain advantages and disadvantages, but all are part of the history of cost-effectiveness and cost-benefit analysis in human services. All of the methods of cost-effectiveness and cost-benefit analysis could benefit from the use of random assignment to different procedures to reduce the possibility that differences in client background are responsible for observed differences in outcomes.

COST → PROCEDURE → OUTCOME RELATIONSHIPS: CROSS TABULATIONS

Interprocedure Comparisons

Tables comparing cost to effectiveness for two alternative procedures or programs are among the earliest methods of attempting to determine which of several programs is better when data are available on both costs and outcomes. Fishman (1975) constructed tables that reflect an either-or approach best suited to choosing between programs after separate statistical analyses of their costs and outcomes. Fishman reasoned that two programs could differ or be similar in outcomes, costs, or both. If the outcomes of Program A were superior to the outcomes of Program B and the costs of Program A were less than the costs of Program B, then Program A is the obvious choice (see Table 5.1). Fishman tables also can be used to contrast the cost and outcome of two alternative treatment procedures that are being considered for implementation within a single-service program.

In the framework provided by Fishman's table, the difficult situation is when one program has better outcomes but also higher costs. Is the improvement in outcome worth the increment in cost? That question is one of values and budget constraints, neither of which are easily integrated into a tabular format such as Fishman's. At least budget considerations can be incorporated into other means of portraying relationships between costs and outcomes, such as the activity analysis model described later in this chapter. The heuristic value of Fishman's table diminishes, too, as we return to problems introduced earlier in this text. For example, with multiple measures of outcomes, it is likely that one program will have better outcomes than another on some measures but not on others. A composite measure of outcome would be required. Similarly, by entertaining a variety of perspectives on what *cost* means, one program may be less costly than another from one perspective but not from a different perspective.

Extension of Fishman's table to three or more programs also seems likely to result in ambiguous decisions about which program is more cost-effective, more cost-beneficial, or to be preferred in funding decisions. For example, Program A would be preferred over Programs B and C only if Program A were superior to B *and* C in effectiveness and less than B *and* C in cost. As more possible trade-offs of cost and outcome become possible, decisions about which program to choose become more difficult.

Finally, it seems important that the *better than* and *inferior to* positions of Programs A and B be determined in some unbiased manner that considers the potential problems of unrepresentative samples and nonsignificant differences before declaring one program's outcomes or costs to be different from another's. The equals sign in Table 5.1 may be seen as meaning *not significantly different according to statistical tests.* This is likely to be accepted for measures of program outcome. Of course, it is similarly crucial to consider the statistical significance of differences in program costs.

Intraprogram Comparisons

Newman Tables

Pre-post tables can be used to examine the effects on outcomes, costs, and processes of a specific therapy procedure, an entire course of therapy, a whole program, or an era. First applied to cost-effectiveness analysis by Carter and Newman (1976; see also Newman & Sorensen, 1985), tables are formed by using measures of outcome, cost, or process that have an ordinal scale or better. Ordered categories can be formed for more sophis-

Table 5.2

Number of Patients in GAS[a] Categories
Before Versus Three Months After Admission

GAS[a] 3 Months Following Admission	GAS[a] at Admission							
	11-20	21-30	31-40	41-50	51-60	61-70	71-80	Totals
11-20	1	0	0	0	0	0	0	1
21-30	0	1	0	1	0	0	0	2
31-40	0	3	0	0	0	0	0	3
41-50	0	4	6	6	0	0	0	16
51-60	3	1	6	19	1	0	0	30
61-70	1	0	4	15	0	0	0	20
71-80	0	0	0	1	0	0	0	1
Totals	5	9	16	42	1	0	0	73

a. Global Assessment Scale.

ticated measures by breaking the numeric output into ranges. For example, improvement on the Global Assessment Scale (Spitzer, Gibbon, & Endicott, 1975) that ranged from 1 to 100 could be segmented into 10-point ranges. Data for the following analyses are from an inpatient program for adolescents who were admitted with DSM diagnoses of either major depression, conduct disorder, or mixed personality dysfunction.

To form a pre-post table, the categories of outcome, cost, or process are listed in order down the rows of the table for measures taken at one time (e.g., prior to the delivery of services). The columns on the pre-post table list the same categories for the same variable but for a different time (e.g., following completion of the delivery of services). The pre-post table in Table 5.2 shows that most patients increased in level of functioning from admission to 3 months following admission. The cells of the table on the diagonal from the upper left corner to the lower right corner indicate no change (within the ranges of the categories used here). Whereas some patients stayed at approximately the same level of functioning, as indicated by nine patients in diagonal cells, many more improved (indicated by the many patients in cells below the diagonal). One patient moved to a lower level of functioning, as indicated by the "1" in the cell of the 41 to 50 range for GAS at admission and the 21 to 30 range for GAS 3 months following admission.

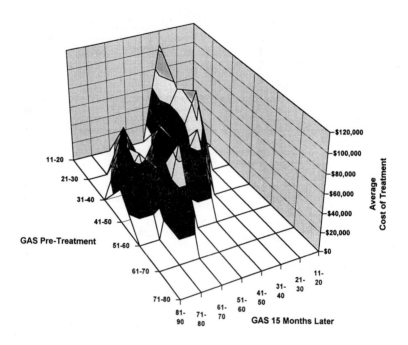

Figure 5.1. Three-Dimensional Newman Cost-Outcome Matrix
NOTE: GAS stands for Global Assessment Scale.

Of course, the pre-post table provides only a rough picture of how much patient functioning changed over the course of therapy. This sort of analysis does not rule out other explanations for the change observed, either, although patients with similar diagnoses may have been shown to have a low rate of so-called spontaneous recovery. Constructing a similar table for a waiting-list control group would offer a superior means of comparing the effects of treatment to the often beneficial effects of the simple passage of time. The problem is, so often, that control groups simply are not available in this sort of setting.

Pre-post tables can be adapted to show the value of resources spent on patients during this period. In this case, a similar amount of resources was spent on each patient because the duration of treatment was similar and all patients stayed in the same facility. If 3 months of treatment cost $9,000 per patient, the average cost of treatment for patients in each cell can be shown. A three-dimensional display of the cost → outcome relationship in this program can be used as well (Figure 5.1).

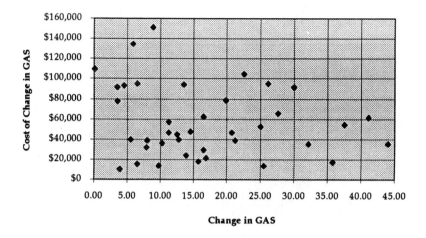

Figure 5.2. Outcomes and Their Costs
NOTE: The outcomes shown are changes on the Global Assessment Scale (GAS).

COST → PROCEDURE → OUTCOME GRAPHS

Outcomes Graphed as a Function of Costs

A two-dimensional representation of this resource → outcome relationship is provided in Figure 5.2, which depicts the relationship between change in GAS and the cost of producing that change. The corresponding costs of treatment differ among patients due to varying durations of treatment. It might be feared that converting the pre-post dimension into a single change dimension risks obscuring relationships between pretreatment, but this concern was allayed somewhat by finding no significant correlation between pretreatment GAS and change in GAS.

The data shown in Figure 5.2 indicate the costs and outcomes of treatment for each patient. This graph is both dismaying in its variability and illuminating, in that a generally negative relationship seems to exist between resources devoted to treatment and change in GAS. The direction of this relationship is, of course, counterintuitive: One would think that if more resources were devoted to treatment, more would come of it. Might more resources be required, however, for treatment of individuals who begin at lower levels of functioning? Graphing cost of treatment against pretreatment GAS suggested that this was not the case, although the

concentration of pretreatment GAS around 40 prevented a definitive con-
clusion regarding this possibility.

Other Relationships Possible Between Costs
and Outcomes and Step Functions

Although diminishing returns are the norm in most economic sectors,
that relationship may hold only if a single and highly efficient technology
is being used in manufacturing (or service). Mental health and health
services seem to employ a variety of competing technologies at once, and
sometimes these mix to generate relationships that deviate from the standard diminishing returns curve.

The dynamic relationships between service procedures and biological or
psychological processes may be such that without a certain minimum level of
resources, there is only a mediocre level of benefit or effectiveness in the
program. Once an additional therapist can be hired, however, or once a new
component or division can be added to a program (e.g., case management,
diagnosis, and assessment), there may be a sudden increase in effectiveness.
Given the uncertainty of most measures of outcomes and resources, graphs of
resource → outcome relationships that have several steps may become difficult
to distinguish from smooth exponential growth functions.

Nonmonotonic and Negative Cost →
Outcome Relationships

A third type of relationship sometimes is found between the resources
used to provide a service and the outcomes produced by that service:
Sometimes less is more. Occasionally, the same psychological, health, or
social problem can be treated using the least costly of several available
procedures with the best outcome of those available procedures.

For example, Bandura, Blanchard, and Ritter (1969) found that the most
effective treatment for snake phobia (participant modeling) also required
the least time from therapists and clients alike. Of clients who received the
participant modeling treatment, 92% performed the terminal step of snake
approach (hands at side while a 3-foot snake rested in the lap for 2 minutes).
This treatment required an average of 2 hours and 10 minutes from clients
and the same time from therapists. Systematic desensitization was only
25% effective on the same outcome measure and required more than twice
the time (a mean 4 hours, 33 minutes). This inverse relationship between
costs and outcome is captured in Figure 5.3. Effectiveness is shown in the
line curve; resources are the bars.

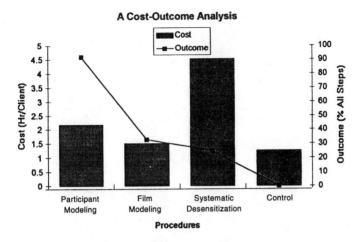

Figure 5.3. A Cost-Outcome Analysis for Snake Phobia Treatment

Of course, all program procedures can be considered to have a more costly alternative that is less likely to be effective. It is easy to imagine some variation on a human service that would take more time or consume other additional resources, with little or no effect on outcomes. For instance, a therapist could meet daily rather than weekly with an obsessive-compulsive client to discuss topics in gardening. The result probably would be lower benefits than in participant modeling but significantly higher costs.

Using Graphs of Cost → Outcome Relationships to Manage Human Services

Perhaps you are thinking, "All these graphs are nice, if you like that sort of thing, but how can they help me make service decisions, justify our funding requests, and defend the budgets?" What they show is how choosing treatments solely on their ratio of cost-to-effectiveness or effectiveness-divided-by-cost could be wrong. Consider, for example, the film modeling procedure shown in Figure 5.3. This treatment has, from the perspective of therapists, almost zero cost because it requires only that the client be shown how to start, stop, and reverse a videotape player (which they probably already knew) and then be left alone to view the tape. Any effectiveness divided by near-zero cost results in a very high effectiveness-to-cost ratio, so film modeling is the most cost-effective treatment, right?

Probably not, and even if it was, it probably is not the one that should be chosen. Including the costs of the VCR and tape plus the cost of office space, administrative assistance, bookkeeping, and other overhead expenses would increase the cost to a significant level even if no therapist time is involved. The cost of film modeling is lower than any treatment procedure, certainly, but it is not zero unless you adopt an exclusively "therapist" perspective. Moreover, a near-perfect outcome is possible only if some additional funds are made available to enable the participant modeling procedure. The desirability of a so-called cure for almost everyone is strong enough that most providers would, ideally, decide to opt for the participant modeling procedure.

Of course, one need not make decisions about service provision in the straitjacket of conceptualizing these procedures as alternatives. Classic outcome research assigns clients randomly to alternative treatments, but clinical decision making that keeps an eye on costs might well assign clients to treatments based on the probability of success. For example, snake phobics might be first assigned to the least expensive treatment that has a definite probability of success (e.g., film modeling). Those who do not achieve a cure with this procedure then could be given the more expensive but probably more effective participant modeling treatment. This decision assumes that receiving film modeling prior to participant modeling would not spoil the effectiveness of the participant modeling. It also assumes that clients who do not benefit from film modeling would be similar to clients who, in the original research, received only participant modeling. These assumptions seem reasonable, according to theories of the etiology of snake phobia, but would have to be tested by assigning clients to video only, video followed by participant modeling, and participant modeling only. The resulting effectiveness and cost data then could be used in the next round of decision making.

Ideally, successive iterations of data collection, analysis, decision making, modification of treatment procedures, and a return to data collection would gradually optimize the cost-effectiveness of treatment. More complex decision making can be conducted using *operations research* procedures (Yates, 1980b; see also Kessler, 1981). These procedures for decision making require considerable data, however, and make a set of assumptions that may not hold in health and mental health service systems.

Constraints on Costs and Outcomes:
Effects on Management Decisions

Graphs of outcomes versus costs represent the maximum outcomes that can be obtained using a particular procedure at different levels of cost.

Cost-effectiveness and cost-benefit decisions are complicated in a different way when constraints on cost, and on outcomes, are considered. Budget limits are familiar constraints on the maximum amounts, and sometimes on the types, of resources that can be consumed by human services. Limits on outcomes also enter into most human service decisions, either explicitly or by assumption: The limits are on the *minimum* levels of outcome that are acceptable.

Funders often set a maximum on the resources that can be devoted to human services, either in negotiation with the human service system or following bids from competing providers. In residential programs, the maximum may be specified as cost per client per unit of service (e.g., per session) or as cost per client per month. Clinics also may receive a lump sum for delivering services to a particular community. Both arrangements create cost maxima that enter into decisions about which programs, approaches, components, or therapists to use. Cost constraints can be represented on graphs of (cost, outcome) data as lines that demark two regions: components that can be used and those that cannot, due to lack of funding.

For example, imagine you have just settled into your office and you find on your desktop cost → outcome curves for three alternative service programs or procedures or change agents, as shown in Figure 5.4. Suppose that these are the results of some extensive analyses by your CPPOA staff of the outcomes of implementing three different procedures (A, B, and C) over substantial ranges of resource expenditures. These procedures may be three treatment procedures that therapists can perform, three entirely different programs, or even three therapists at the same program. By determining one's budget and then examining the graph, a manager could decide which program, procedure, or therapist would be most effective for the level of funding available. If the budget was Y (toward the middle of the horizontal cost axis in Figure 5.4), for example, A or B would yield better outcomes than C. If the budget were increased to Z, then A would be chosen over B and C. If the budget were decreased to X, then C would be preferred.

Given these findings, can a prescription be made for which program to use in general? One might think that Program A would be best. Figure 5.4 might suggest to some decision makers, however, that Program C might be better: At the lower range of costs (below X on the cost axis), C is superior in outcomes to A and B (chiefly because neither A nor B can be afforded at the lower costs shown in this figure). Thus, graphing this particular set of cost-outcome relationships allows decisions that control costs and optimize effectiveness within current budget constraints, and allows decision makers to anticipate how much outcome could be improved by increasing the budget limit (for additional examples, see Siegert & Yates, 1980; Yates, 1978).

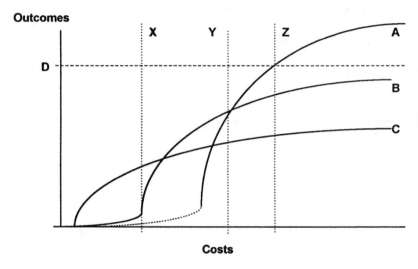

Figure 5.4. Cost → Outcome Functions for Three Alternative Service Procedures

Managers can use the graphed lines in Figure 5.4 to make another sort of management decision. If one is committed to using a particular program, procedure, or change agent (whatever the lines represent), the level of funding at which it generates the greatest effectiveness can be determined by looking at the graph. Some, such as Line A, will generate better outcomes only at high levels of funding (i.e., above Y). Others, such as Line B, require a certain minimum level of funding before appreciable outcomes can occur. Depending on one's level of funding, and if there were not a constraint on minimum outcome, the manager might switch from procedure C to B to A as funding increased to the point where superior outcomes could be achieved with the next procedure. In a way, then, the envelope of curves C, B, and A forms the cost-outcome relationship to be considered by the managers.

A qualification needs to be made, however, if the (cost, outcome) data pairs that were used to plot the lines did not come from a long-term study during which the same program, procedure, or change agent received different levels of funding. If these (cost, outcome) coordinates were obtained at a single point in time from different programs, approaches, or therapists, the sort of decision making described may not result in the predicted cost-outcome relationship due to a confounding of funding level with program, procedure, or change agent. If the programs are similar in some way, it is reasonable to connect the dots produced by graphing the costs and outcomes of individual programs. The programs may differ, however, in ways that are not readily apparent but that may produce higher or lower levels of outcomes once funding is modified to the level corresponding to another program on the same line. In sum, one has to be more cautious when making decisions that use cost-outcome data obtained cross-sectionally from different programs, approaches, or therapists. At the very least, it would be important to monitor the results of an increase or decrease in funding to see whether the predicted change in outcome was achieved.

In addition to this possible constraint on maximum outcomes attainable, there may be a minimum level of outcome that is acceptable. It is relatively easy to find outcomes that are in the unacceptable region. It generally would be unacceptable, for example, if only 1% of clients maintained smoking cessation at a 6-month posttreatment follow-up. It is more difficult to determine where the dividing line is between acceptable and unacceptable outcome. For example, is a 40% abstinence rate at 3 years following treatment satisfactory for alcohol abuse? Is 20% long-term abstinence OK? Relative to cost constraints, outcome constraints are more difficult to establish with reliability and validity. Minimum acceptable effectiveness or benefits could be determined empirically by surveying interest groups for definitions of what changes would be the minimum they would find acceptable. (*Acceptable* might mean "will pay for" in some communities and "will not sue for" in others.) In deciding whether to adopt a new treatment procedure, outcome constraints also could be set as the outcomes demonstrated by procedures currently in use. In Figure 5.4, an outcome constraint could be represented by a horizontal line such as D. The outcome constraint line intersects the vertical outcome axis at the minimum acceptable outcome. Using this outcome constraint, procedures C and B are not acceptable at any budget level despite their lower cost relative to A.

Funders may require specific minimum outcome levels, but they typically are more concerned with costs. It is common, in fact, for government funders to assume that human services offered by different providers using different procedures result in essentially identical outcomes. Competitions among service providers then are based primarily on cost per patient. Outcomes may be mentioned, but the specific procedures used are more likely to be described. The space devoted to outcomes in the social service proposal usually is small relative to descriptions of procedures and resource expenditures planned. Perhaps this will change as data on outcomes are collected more routinely as the scientist-manager-practitioner role becomes the norm rather than the exception in human service administration.

Statistical Comparisons

Graphic models of cost-outcome relationships go a long way toward depicting cost-effectiveness and cost-benefit relationships in ways that can be used by managers to make decisions about the best way to offer human services in changing, challenging economic environments. It would be a mistake, however, to assume that every difference visible between two lines graphed from a cloud of cost-outcome coordinates was a valid difference that should lead to changes in human service delivery. The concepts of statistical significance that usually are applied to the outcomes of human services need to be considered in the arenas of costs and cost-outcome relationships, too.

For graphic models, this means that if a difference between points graphed for alternative programs, agents, or service components would cause a change in service procedures, that difference should be tested statistically prior to changing procedures (e.g., Siegert & Yates, 1980). For pre-post tables, there needs to be a comparison of the changes in outcome that would be expected by chance. Differences between patterns of change in pre-post tables that were caused by the specific procedures of treatment, and not by factors external to the service system, should be examined statistically too. If ratios of outcomes to costs (e.g., benefit-to-cost ratios) are used, they, too, can be compared statistically. For statistical comparisons of ratios, outcome and cost data need to be collected on units of service that are more detailed than the units being compared. For example, if the cost-benefits of two programs are being compared, the relative cost-benefit of each could be described using cost-benefit ratios or benefit-cost differences calculated for each client in each program. (Often, evaluators report only a single benefit-to-cost ratio for an entire program, even though they would seldom measure outcomes for the program as a whole.) Separate benefit-to-cost ratios for each client would allow assessment of the variance in cost-benefit for the programs, enabling the use of parametric statistics such as t tests. In this way, the nature of the cost $\rightarrow$ procedure $\rightarrow$ outcome relationship could be examined: The t test would indicate which procedure generated superior outcomes for each unit cost.

Nonparametric tests of the cost-outcome relationships in competing programs are possible as well. The benefit-cost relationship could be assessed separately for each client, and the number of clients whose benefits exceeded costs could be tabulated along with the number of clients whose costs exceeded benefits. If there was uncertainty about whether certain clients' benefits were greater or less than their costs, a third group could be created. Then the numbers in these tables could be contrasted with a nonparametric test, such as χ^2. Of course, more than two programs could be compared using this strategy.

ACTIVITY ANALYSIS AND NETWORK MODELS OF OPTIMIZING COST → PROCEDURE → PROCESS → OUTCOME RELATIONSHIPS

Graphs and, to a lesser degree, ratios, differences, and tables are all ways of describing relationships between costs and outcomes. When a different ratio, table, or graph is constructed for each procedure or process and they are compared, managers can make more informed decisions about which procedure to implement to achieve which process. Adding information on cost and outcome constraints helps managers' decisions be more realistic. The information can quickly become so detailed, though, that it is overwhelming. When specific constraints are placed on each of several types of resources and when alternative procedures yield different outcomes after consuming varying amounts of each resource, it becomes difficult to use ratios, tables, or graphs to make the necessary decisions. In these instances, a more complex model than can be provided by ratios, tables, or even graphs is needed.

Tested approaches to developing models of service systems that facilitate management decisions are provided by operations research (Häfner & Wolfram, 1991; Hillier & Lieberman, 1974; Kessler, 1981). The most frequently used method of constructing and analyzing data on resources, procedures, outcomes, and resource constraints is *linear programming*. Yates (1980b) describes several potential applications of operations research methods to optimize the delivery of human services.

Linear programming is particularly good at finding the most effective combination of service procedures in situations that present a variety of client problems that must be solved on a tight budget. If one procedure is shown to be the most effective and least expensive according to controlled clinical research, the solution is easy: Spend all resources on that procedure. Different problems often are best solved by different procedures, however. To maximize the longevity of a population, for example, one cannot simply force everyone to exercise. Diet, drug use, stress, and many other factors codetermine how long one lives. Moreover, there are limits to the amounts of time, energy, money, and skill that individuals can use in efforts to prolong their lives. There are constraints, too, on the availability of health professionals to help people in efforts to change their behavior, cognition, and affect in healthy ways. How does one cope with all the complexities of this problem? We all do, at an individual level and with informal decision rules. Linear programming offers a more structured way to proceed, whether the analysis is conducted at the level of the individual or groups of individuals for whom similar cost → procedure → process → outcome relationships hold.

Building a Quantitative Model of Costs, Procedures, Processes, and Outcomes

The first step in linear programming is the hardest and most costly: conducting the research to build a databased model of the problem. This has been the focus of most of the book. Usually, evaluation research stops after measuring the resources, procedures, processes, and outcomes. This is where operations research begins. Continuing the longevity maximization example, we could use the activity analysis framework for linear programming that is shown in Table 5.3. This framework guides the assembly of information on what procedures (second row from the top) will be used to modify the biological, behavioral, cognitive, and affective processes (top row) that determine how long individuals in the target population live (according to basic and applied research).

In the columns, Table 5.3 presents only a subset of the health-related behaviors, cognitions, and affects that are typically recommended for maximizing longevity. The interest group perspective used in assembling these hypothetical data is that of a health enhancement program. Client time and client money are considered, not because they are a responsibility of the program but because the program wishes to consider client constraints on time and money to minimize dropouts.

Some of the principal resources that would be used in a longevity enhancement program are listed in the rows. The leftmost cell in each row describes the units in which the resources are measured: Note that these need not be expressed in monetary units. Instead, the units that are most intrinsic to the resource and its procedure should be used. The rightmost cell in each row indicates the constraint on the resource.

The next-to-last row shows the estimated (and hypothetical) yield that each procedure of the health enhancement program would produce in added years of life if it were successful. The bottom row lists the probability of success—the effectiveness—of the procedure in achieving the outcome. These data reflect process → outcome relationships, and they are portrayed here as static. Actually, they would vary depending on (a) the other components of health enhancement that were implemented and (b) the current health status of the individual. These figures assume that one to two other components are implemented.

A final set of constraints was added in recognition of the manner in which most health promotion services are offered: Either you use the service or you don't. There's no halfway point (unless one considers partial participation in a program). These constraints were placed on the implementation of program components: The degree of implementation was required to be either 0% or 100%. A more complex analysis might, of course, wish to allow a range of values between 0% and 100%. This would recognize that some clients do indeed vary their participation within the constraints of many other demands on their time. Money, practitioner time, and other resources, however, would have to be allocated in a 0% or 100% fashion.

This table is meant as an example only: It has been constructed for a person who has a number of poor health habits that need improvement. A different table with different entries in the cells would be constructed for individuals with healthier behavior patterns. In addition, space has been treated the same way, whereas space for medical examinations and related services can be considerably more expensive than space for other activities, such as exercise.

A more sophisticated linear programming model would have dynamic outcome indices, which would vary as a function of interactions between changes in various processes and the net effect on expected lifetime length. For example, if smoking continued, even the change from Type A to Type B styles might not produce an increment of more than 1 or 2 years, whereas changing both could improve lifetime duration by over a decade. In all likelihood, each additional effort at health enhancement would have somewhat less of an effect than previous health enhancement, leading to diminishing returns on the health enhancement investment.

Solving the Cost → Procedure → Process → Outcome Model
for the Most Cost-Effective or Cost-Beneficial Solution

Linear programming now is a common procedure in most business software packages; they also come with some standard spreadsheet programs, such as Microsoft's Excel©, available for a variety of computing platforms (e.g., IBM-compatible and Macintosh® computers). Table 5.3 translates the data in Table 5.2 into a format more amenable to conducting linear programming and seeing the results. This is the layout of data that, when made on a spreadsheet, allows solution of the matrix for optimal outcomes within cost constraints. The solution was produced in less than

Table 5.3
Linear Programming Solution for Optimal Cost-Effectiveness: Longevity Maximization[a]

Processes for Improving Longevity →	Regular Use of Professional Health Services	Regular Aerobic Exercise	Cessation of Tobacco Use	Optimistic Explanatory Style	Type B, not Type A[b]	Support Network
Procedures for achieving the processes →	Service awareness training, contact contract	"Heavy Breathing Is Good" tape and training	"Stop Smoking Now! Again!" module	Short-term individual therapy	"Live to work; work so you live" counseling	Social skills training modules

Resources							Resource Limits
Client time (hours per week available for health enhancement)	4 visits annually of about 2 hours each	5 hours of exercise over 7 days = .72 hr/day	1 hour daily for 2 weeks; additional hour per week for first year	0.5 hour per week for 4 weeks, individual therapy	0.875 hour per week for 4 weeks, individual therapy	1.5 hours per week for 6 weeks in social skills training	No more than 6 hours in any given week
Client money (per year, for longevity enhancement)	$200 per month per person (health insurance)	$100 first month, then $30 monthly for equipment, training, classes, or club	$250 for first 2 weeks of program, then $10 per month for the rest of the first year	$100 per hour; $200 total	$175 total	$150 for training	$3,500 total for the year

Health specialist time (reported per client)	3 contacts, 1 hour each	0.5 hours per week per client	0.5 hour weekly for 2 weeks (group meeting); additional 0.25 hour per week for first year	0.5 hour per week for 4 weeks	1 hour per week for 4 weeks	0.25 hours weekly for 6 weeks	18 hours per client per year
Health assistant time (reported per client)	4 visits, 1 hour per visit	1 hour per week per client	1 hour daily for 2 weeks; additional 1 hour per week for first year	0.25 hours	0.20 hours	1 hour weekly for 6 weeks	1.5 hours per client per week
Room hours (a measure of space available)	1 room hour per visit, 4 visits per year	1 room hour each week (shared)	1 room hour (shared) for first month only	2 room-month hours total	2 room-month hours total	0.75 room-month hours (group room) for 1.5 months	60 room hours per client per year
Contribution of procedure to longevity enhancement (years of life added)	5	4	7	2	3	2	
Probability of success	0.85	0.67	0.61	0.45	0.57	0.75	

a. This example shows linear programming to maximize longevity given budget constraints (resource limits) and technological constraints (effectiveness of procedures to enhance longevity).

b. Worked on with optimistic explanatory style.

a minute by highlighting the rows with numbers and pulling down the Tools menu and clicking on Solver. This brought up a simple form that could be completed largely by highlighting different areas of the Table 5.3 spreadsheet. A variety of options could be clicked on or off as well, including maximization (e.g., of outcomes) or minimization (e.g., of health risks or of costs). A new worksheet was generated by the analysis showing which procedures and resources were used fully, which were used partially, and which were not used at all. This information could be used in subsequent cycles of linear programming to find out which resource constraints could be tightened with no discernible effect on outcome and which resource constraints could be slackened by transferring funds to purchase more of the critical resources.

In the transition from Table 5.3 to Table 5.4, a row was inserted following each type of resource. The inserted row shows the actual amount of the resource used, according to the solution. The total actually used is shown in the rightmost cell in this row. A column was inserted to the left of the constraints column to show the total amount of each resource that was used. Another row was added at the bottom of the table to show the actual lifetime increment expected, depending on whether the component was executed or not in the linear programming solution.

The maximum lifetime increment (11.24 years; rightmost cell in the bottom row) that was possible within the resource constraints is the sum of the increments produced by each component that was implemented in the solution. Due to the various resources demanded by the different components, their relative contributions to longevity, and the probability that implementing a component would result in change, only three of the six components were recommended for implementation: (a) use of professional medical services, (b) cessation of tobacco use, and (c) social support network building.

To make the situation more complex (and more realistic), it is possible to identify different subgroups in the population that would benefit from different longevity regimens. These groups could be defined according to age, gender, race, social class, and the presence of existing medical problems. One virtue of linear programming via computer is the ease with which the CPPOA scientist can examine the effects on outcomes of different assumptions, such as the resource mixes needed to implement a procedure. This is just one example of how computer manipulation of models that include data on costs, procedures, processes, and outcomes can aid management of service delivery.

Table 5.4

Expanded Linear Programming Solution for Optimal Cost-Effectiveness: Longevity Maximization

Processes for Improving Longevity →	Regular Use of Professional Health Services	Regular Aerobic Exercise	Cessation of Tobacco Use	Optimistic Explanatory Style	Type B, not Type A[a]	Support Network		
Procedures for achieving the processes →	Service awareness training, contact contract	"Heavy Breathing Is Good" tape and training	"Stop Smoking Now! Again!" module	Short-term individual therapy	"Live to work; work so you live" counseling	Social skills training modules		
Resources							Sum	Resource Limits
Client time (hours per week)	0.15	5.00	1.23	0.04	0.07	0.17		6.00
Client time used	0.15	0.00	1.23	0.00	0.00	0.17	1.56	
Client money (per year)	$2,400	$430	$370	$200	$175	$150		$3,500
Client money used	$2,400	—	$370	—	—	$150	$2,920	
Health specialist time (per client)	3.0	0.5	13.5	2.0	4.0	1.5		18.0
Health specialist time used	3.0	0.0	13.5	0.0	0.0	1.5	18.0	
Health assistant time (per client)	4.0	52.0	64.0	0.25	0.2	6.0		78
Health assistant time used	4.0	52.0	64.0	0.0	0.0	6.0	74.0	
Room hours (space available)	4.0	52.0	1.0	2.0	3.5	1.13		60
Room hours used	4.0	0.0	1.0	0.0	0.0	1.13	6.13	
Potential contribution of procedure	5	4	9	2	3	2		15
Probability of success	0.85	0.67	0.61	0.45	0.57	0.75		
Done?	1	0	1	0	0	1		
Longevity increment (years)	4.25	0.0	5.49	0.0	0.0	1.50		11.24

a. Worked on with optimistic explanatory style.

131

Why Processes Still Need to Be
Considered in Linear Programming

Mental health and health services seldom are delivered in the same way regardless of the client's problem or diagnosis. In the context of CPPOA, treatment procedures usually are not administered regardless of the psychological and biological processes that are occurring in the individual. Rather, the nature of the problem determines the treatment procedures that are used. The matching of problem to procedure determines the rest of the CPPOA equation. Certainly, the procedures chosen determine the resources that will be needed. The procedure addresses specific psychological and other processes related to the client's problem. The interaction of these processes and the problem along with uncontrollable factors in the client's physical and social environment produce the outcomes of treatment.

For example, Gray and Shields (1992) suggest that treatment outcomes will be maximum if different treatment procedures are used for clients who are at different phases of the process through which they may respond to separation and divorce. In the first phase (urge to recover the lost object), Gray and Shields suggest attending a support group for people experiencing separation or divorce. This treatment should, according to Gray and Shields, help clients express their urge and learn from others about the desirability of attempting to return to the relationship versus moving forward. If the first phase's processes take longer than a few months, the addition of individual therapy to the support group experience is proposed.

A different treatment procedure—intensive individual therapy—is recommended for clients in the second phase of separation or divorce—disorganization. This is suggested because the psychological processes at this stage may include clinical depression with occasional suicidal ideation. For the third phase, reorganization, short-term therapy and subsequent support group work is recommended to facilitate the healing processes of integrating separation and divorce into one's life. Prochaska and colleagues have, as noted in an earlier chapter, found that the outcomes of treatment procedures depend substantially on the particular phase at which a client currently resides—the processes currently active in the client (Prochaska et al., 1994).

Clearly, then, the processes within the client are important in determining which procedure will produce the best outcomes. Information on the cost → procedure → process → outcome relationships can be incorporated indirectly into linear programming by developing different activity analysis matrices (such as Table 5.3) for each phase of the process. Entirely different cost → procedure → process → outcome linkages may be in effect, depending on where the client is in the process. Alternatively, more flexible and more complex models can be used to integrate this information, as will be described.

Service Network Models: Describing Cost →
Procedure → Process → Outcome Linkages

From Activity Analysis to Network Analysis

Activity analysis models capture important aspects of cost → procedure → process → outcome linkages and allow ready solution of problems in resource allocation among service procedures. Important assumptions can be obscured, however, by the activity analysis approach. Subtle relationships between procedures and myriad processes may be buried in numbers or entirely ignored. Finally, the uncertainty of the research findings used in the activity analysis matrix is not always made explicit.

To take into account the variability of the strength (and direction) of relationships between costs, procedures, processes, and outcomes, an alternative model is a *directional network*. Figure 5.5 provides a network model for the hypothetical program analyzed earlier with linear programming. A network model can represent resources as different nodes; procedures, processes, and outcomes also can be conceptualized as other sets of nodes in the same network. Figure 5.5 indicates these different categories of nodes by using different shapes to depict each (e.g., resource nodes are rectangular, whereas procedure nodes are oval or circular).

The links between nodes show that relationships exist between different nodes. The strength of these relationships can be expressed by numbers attached to the links or by the width of the links. Relationships that are hypothesized but not found to be statistically significant can be shown by the absence of a link between the entities that might have been involved in the relationship. For example, the top cost → procedure link (between Client Time and Regular Use of Health Services) has a number associated with it that shows the average hours required of clients for that procedure (0.15 hours per week). The link between the procedure Regular Use of Health Services and the process Enable Medical Technologies to Have Maximum Effect shows the strength of this probabilistic relationship (.85) as indicated by (hypothetical) research that measured the intermediate effect of the procedure. Finally, the relationship between the process Enabling Medical Technologies to Have Maximum Effect and the outcome Longevity Enhancement is expressed by the expected increment in years of life (5 years). Of course, the process → outcome relationship is itself probabilistic: The value—5 years—is the

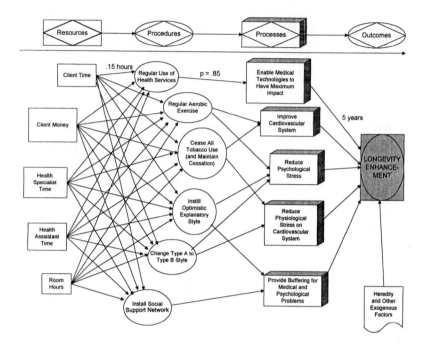

Figure 5.5. Partial Path Analysis Format for Cost → Procedure → Process → Outcome Analysis

result of a probability of the outcome being achieved in an environment that presents an array of other factors that may mitigate or enhance the relationship between a process and an outcome.

Basic and applied researchers have long used network models to express and test how much each of a multitude of factors (e.g., unemployment, access to inexpensive drugs, role modeling of substance abuse by a parent) contributes to complex behaviors, such as substance abuse (Chassin, Presson, Sherman, & Edwards, 1991). *Path analysis* is a statistical method of analyzing large data sets to establish these linkages (James, Mulaik, & Brett, 1982). Relatively inexpensive computer programs are available that make path analysis accessible to most researchers (e.g., EzPATH®; Steiger, 1989; similar analytic options are available for other popular statistical software, such as SPSS® and SAS®).

Constraints on resources, including budget limits, can be expressed as limits on the capacity of a link to convey more than, say, a set number of clients from one point to another within a given period of time. Operations research methods, such as linear programming, can then be used to find the optimum path through the complex network of cost → procedure → process → outcome relationships. *Optimum* could be defined, for solution, as "costs no more than X" or "achieved at least Y outcome at the lowest possible cost."

Constructing Network Models
in a Single-Service System

This sort of network model can be developed by correlational analyses of data from a single-service system, although ideally it is constructed from analyses of data from a representative variety of systems. The focus of the preceding analyses has been primarily on relationships between resources and outcomes. The effects of service procedures on outcomes and costs has been examined somewhat indirectly: Different graphs, different tables, or different ratios were to be constructed for each procedure. This fits with one way in which psychological and other services often are provided: as alternatives from among which a service manager must choose and as packages that are implemented on an all-or-none basis. For example, when choosing between different methods of teaching parents how to manage their children's misbehavior, one could choose either in-office or in-home delivery of child management training. Thus, a variety of different treatments can be considered and the relationships between which treatment was used and what outcomes were achieved can be quantified.

More often, however, managers of human services consider the degree to which they will offer or implement different services. Also, each service may be composed of a mixture of components, each of which may itself vary in the degree to which it is presented to clients by change agents. The degree of implementation of a service can be reflected in the number of sessions per week or per month, the duration of each contact, whether that contact is more or less intensely focused (e.g., individual or group therapy), and what percentage of the targeted operations were performed during a service contact. Because there is variability across service systems, across therapists within service systems, and even among clients receiving the same type of service from the same therapist in the same system, the degree to which a service is implemented can vary. If service procedures can be considered to exist on a continuum and if outcomes are considered to also be able to vary, then the relationship between procedure implementation and outcomes can be captured with correlations and related analyses.

In addition to degree of implementation, a given service can be separated into discrete components, some of which can be operated independently. Thus, child management training can be provided by meeting monthly, weekly, or daily with a therapist, and that training can be composed of (a) training in use of reinforcement procedures, (b) social skills training, (c) assertiveness exercises, (d) cognitive coping skills, (e) methods of controlling aggression, (f) relapse prevention training, or several different combinations of these components. The presence or absence of each component may have a measurable effect on outcomes, as may the degree to which each component of the service is implemented. Thus, the sort of analyses described earlier can be performed within individual service systems to optimize their cost-effectiveness and cost-benefit.

Epilogue:
Keeping Down the Cost of CPPOA

Having made it this far, you may be both enthused about the potential of CPPOA and concerned about its cost. It would be hypocritical to analyze and attempt to improve the cost-effectiveness and cost-benefit of social services systems and refuse to do the same for one's own evaluation services. But what is the alternative to the sort of CPPOA detailed in the preceding chapters?

Let me propose not an alternative to, but a "lite" version of CPPOA that might approximate the effectiveness of full CPPOA at lower cost. It is possible that estimation of relationships between costs, procedures, processes, and outcomes by persons who are very familiar with the service system could yield a model of subjectively weighted cost → procedure → process → outcome linkages that would be about as good a fit as the more objective model we would have constructed with much effort over a long period of time. This, of course, is an empirical question—of the cost-effectiveness of alternative methods of constructing cost → procedure → process → outcome models.

Once a model of CPPOA relationships is constructed, it needs to be manipulated to show how treatment costs can be minimized, treatment outcomes maximized, or both. It is possible that manipulation of CPPOA models to show how to achieve the best outcomes and the lowest costs can be conducted about as effectively with intuitive procedures as with complex operations research methods. Experienced, successful managers who constantly try to improve outcomes within serious constraints of resources and procedures may be especially adept at this sort of manipulation. Certainly, CPPOA should consider this and other ways to minimize its own costs and maximize its targeted outcomes. Those outcomes are the careful measurement and manipulation of relationships between resources expended, procedures performed, processes occurring, and outcomes achieved so that we can deliver, to the best of our ability, the best services to the most people with the greatest need at the lowest possible cost (Yates, 1980b, 1995).

References

Alinsky, S. D. (1971). *Rules for radicals.* Chicago: University of Chicago Press.

Anastasi, A. (1976). *Psychological testing.* New York: Macmillan.

Anderson, D. R., Sweeney, D. J., & Williams, T. A. (1976). *An introduction to management science: Quantitative approaches to decision making.* St. Paul, MN: West.

Andreasen, N. C. (1991). Assessment issues and the cost of schizophrenia. *Schizophrenia Bulletin, 17,* 455-481.

Anglin, M. D., Hser, Y. I., & Chou, C. P. (1993). Reliability and validity of retrospective behavioral self-report by narcotics addicts. *Evaluation Review, 17,* 91-108.

Angoff, W. H. (1988). The nature-nurture debate, aptitudes, and group differences. *American Psychologist, 43,* 713-720.

Aspinwall, L. G., Kemeny, M. E., Taylor, S. E., Schneider, S. G., & Dudley, J. P. (1991). Psychosocial predictors of gay men's AIDS risk-reduction behavior. *Health Psychology, 10,* 432-444.

Azrin, N. H., Philip, R. A., Thienes-Hontas, P., & Basalel, V. A. (1980). Comparative evaluation of the Job Club program with welfare recipients. *Journal of Vocational Behavior, 16,* 133-145.

Bandura, A. (1978). The self system in reciprocal determinism. *American Psychologist, 33,* 344-358.

Bandura, A. (1982). Self-efficacy mechanism in human agency. *American Psychologist, 37,* 122-147.

Bandura, A., Adams, N. E., & Beyer, J. (1977). Cognitive processes mediating behavioral change. *Journal of Personality and Social Psychology, 35,* 125-139.

Bandura, A., Blanchard, E. B., & Ritter, B. (1969). Relative efficacy of desensitization and modeling approaches for inducing behavioral, affective, and attitudinal changes. *Journal of Personality and Social Psychology, 13,* 173-199.

Bandura, A., Cioffi, D., Taylor, C. B., & Brouillard, M. E. (1987). Perceived self-efficacy in coping with cognitive stressors and opioid activation. *Journal of Personality and Social Psychology, 55,* 479-488.

Barlow, D. H., Hayes, S. C., & Nelson, R. O. (1984). *The scientist practitioner: Research and accountability in clinical and educational settings.* New York: Pergamon.

Bass, R. F. (1987). Computer-assisted observer training. *Journal of Applied Behavior Analysis, 20,* 83-88.

Beck, A. T. (1961). An inventory for measuring depression. *Archives of General Psychiatry, 4,* 541-571.

Beecham, J., Knapp, M., & Fenyo, A. (1991). Costs, needs, and outcomes. *Schizophrenia Bulletin, 17,* 427-439.

Bickman, L. (Ed.). (1987). *Using program theory in evaluation* (New Directions for Program Evaluation, No. 33). San Francisco: Jossey-Bass.

Bickman, L., Hedrick, T. E., & Rog, D. J. (1993). *Applied research design: A practical guide.* Newbury Park, CA: Sage.

Bloom, H. S. (1995). Minimum detectable effects: A simple way to report the statistical power of experimental designs. *Evaluation Review, 19,* 547-556.

Bluementhal, S. J. (1988). Suicide: A guide to risk factors, assessment, and treatment of suicidal patients. *Medical Clinics of North America, 72,* 937-971.

Booth-Kewley, S., & Friedman, H. S. (1987). Psychological predictors of heart disease: A quantitative review. *Psychological Bulletin, 101,* 343-362.

Brady, R. (1987). A new method for the computerized delivery of liquid methadone to substance abusers. In J. Lieff (Ed.), *Computers in Psychiatry.* New York: Psychiatric Press.

Calsyn, R. J., Allen, G., Morse, G. A., Smith, R., & Tempelhoff, B. (1993). Can you trust self-report data provided by homeless mentally ill individuals? *Evaluation Review, 17,* 353-366.

Campbell, D. T., & Stanley, J. C. (1963). *Experimental and quasi-experimental designs for research.* Chicago: Rand McNally.

Carter, D. E., & Newman, F. L. (1976). *A client-oriented system of mental health service delivery and program management: A workbook and guide* (DHEW Publication No. ADM 76-307). Rockville, MD: National Institute of Mental Health.

Carver, C. S., & Scheier, M. F. (1981). *Attention and self-regulation: A control-theory approach to human behavior.* New York: Springer-Verlag.

Chan, Y. L., & Sullivan, R. S. (1986). *Quantitative systems for business.* Englewood Cliffs, NJ: Prentice Hall.

Chassin, L., Presson, C. C., Sherman, S. J., & Edwards, D. A. (1991). Four pathways to young-adult smoking status: Adolescent social-psychological antecedents in a midwestern community sample. *Health Psychology, 10,* 409-418.

Chen, H. (1990). *Theory driven evaluations.* Newbury Park, CA: Sage.

Cohen, J. (1965). Some statistical issues in psychological research. In B. B. Wolman (Ed.), *Handbook of clinical psychology* (pp. 95-121). New York: McGraw-Hill.

Cohen, J. (1988). *Statistical power analysis for the behavioral sciences* (2nd ed.). Hillsdale, NJ: Lawrence Erlbaum.

Cohen, J. (1990). Things I have learned (so far). *American Psychologist, 45,* 1304-1312.

Cook, J. A. (1992, November). *Modeling staff perceptions of a mobile job support program for persons with severe mental illness.* Paper presented at the annual meeting of the American Evaluation Association, Seattle, WA.

Cook, T. D., & Campbell, D. T. (1979). *Quasi-experimentation: Design and analysis issues for field settings.* Chicago: Rand McNally.

Cronbach, L. J. (1982). *Designing evaluations of educational and social programs.* San Francisco: Jossey-Bass.

Cronbach, L. J., & Furby, L. (1970). How should we measure "change" or should we? *Psychological Bulletin, 74,* 68-80.

Cummings, N. A., Pallak, M. S., Dorken, H., & Henke, C. J. (1992). *The impact of psychological services on medical utilization and costs* (HCFA Contract No. 11-C-98344/9). Baltimore: Health Care Financing Administration.

Dallal, G. E. (1988). DESIGN: A supplementary module for SYSTAT and SYGRAPH (Version 3.1). Evanston, IL: SYSTAT.

Davis, F. W., & Yates, B. T. (1982). Client level of functioning: Client versus therapist ratings of client level of functioning before and during therapy. *Evaluation and the Health Professions, 5,* 437-448.

Davis, F. W., & Yates, B. T. (1983). Collecting mental health self-evaluations: Effectiveness and cost of three third-party techniques. *Evaluation and the Health Professions, 6*(1), 91-97.

Davis, J. E. (1992). Reconsidering the use of race as an explanatory variable in program evaluation. In A. M. Madison (Ed.), *Minority issues in program evaluation* (New Directions for Program Evaluation, No. 53, pp. 55-67). San Francisco: Jossey-Bass.

Davis, K. E., & Frank, R. G. (1992). Integrating costs and outcomes. In L. Bickman & D. J. Rog (Eds.), *Evaluating mental health services for children* (New Directions for Program Evaluation, No. 54, pp. 55-67). San Francisco: Jossey-Bass.

Delrina Technology. (1992). *WinFax PRO user's guide* (Version 3.0, 1st ed.). San Jose, CA: Author.

DeMuth, N. M., Yates, B. T., & Coates, T. (1984). Psychologists as managers: Old guilts, innovative applications, and pathways to being an effective managerial psychologist. *Professional Psychology, 15,* 758-768.

Diamond, P. M., & Schnee, S. B. (1991). *Lives in the shadows: Some of the costs and consequences of a "non-system" of care.* Austin: Texas University, Hogg Foundation for Mental Health. (ERIC Clearinghouse No. CG 023 819)

Eck, R. D. (1976). *Operations research for business.* Belmont, CA: Wadsworth.

Edwards, W., & Newman, J. R. (1982). *Multiattribute evaluation.* Beverly Hills, CA: Sage.

Elkin, I., Parloff, M. B., Hadley, S. W., & Autry, J. H. (1985). NIMH treatment of depression collaborative research program. *Archives of General Psychiatry, 42,* 305-316.

Embretson, S. W. (1992). Computerized adaptive testing: Its potential substantial contributions to psychological research and assessment. *Current Directions in Psychological Science, 1,* 129-131.

Endicott, J., Spitzer, R., Fleiss, J., & Cohen, J. (1976). The Global Assessment Scale: A procedure for measuring overall severity of psychiatric disturbance. *Archives of General Psychiatry, 33,* 766-771.

Fairweather, G. W., & Davidson, W. S. (1986). *An introduction to community experimentation: Theories, methods, and practice.* New York: McGraw-Hill.

Fairweather, G. W., Sanders, D. H., Maynard, H., & Cressler, D. L. (1969). *Community life for the mentally ill.* Chicago: Aldine.

Fiedler, J. L., & Wight, J. B. (1989). *The medical offset effect and public health policy: Mental health industry in transition.* New York: Praeger.

Filipczak, J., & Yates, B. T. (1989, May 31). *Cost-process outcome assessment in ICFs/MR.* Paper presented at the 113th Annual Meeting of the American Association on Mental Retardation, Chicago.

Fishman, D. B. (1975). Development of a generic cost-effectiveness methodology for evaluating patient services of a community mental health center. In J. Zusman & C. R. Wurster (Eds.), *Evaluation in alcohol, drug abuse, and mental health service* (p. 153ff). Lexington, MA: Heath.

Flynn, P. M., Hubbard, R. L., Forsyth, B. H., Fountain, D. L., & Smith, T. K. (1992, August). *Individual Assessment Profile (IAP): Standardizing the assessment of substance abusers.* Paper presented at the annual meeting of the American Psychological Association, Washington, DC.

Flynn, P. M., Luckey, J. W., Brown, B. S., Hoffman, J. A., Dunteman, G. H., Theisen, A. C., Hubbard, R. L., Needle, R., Schneider, S. J., Koman, J. J., III, Karson, S., Palsgrove, G. L., & Yates, B. T. (1995). Relationship between drug preference and indicators of psychiatric treatment. *American Journal of Drug and Alcohol Abuse, 21*(2), 153-166.

Fowler, F., Jr. (1993). *Survey research methods* (2nd ed., Applied Social Research Methods Series, Vol. 1). Newbury Park, CA: Sage.

Fowler, F. J., Jr., & Mangione, T. W. (1989). *Standardized survey interviewing: Minimizing interviewer-related error* (Applied Social Research Methods Series, Vol. 18). Newbury Park, CA: Sage.

Fox, J. A. (1986). *Randomized response: A method for sensitive surveys.* Beverly Hills, CA: Sage.

Frank, J. D. (1973). *Persuasion and healing: A comparative study of psychotherapy* (2nd ed.). Baltimore: Johns Hopkins University Press.

Frank, J. D. (1982). Therapeutic components shared by all psychotherapies. In J. J. Harvey & M. M. Parkes (Eds.), *Psychotherapy research and behavior change* (Vol. 1). Washington, DC: American Psychological Association.

Franks, D. D. (1987). *The high cost of caring: Economic contribution of families to the care of the mentally ill.* Unpublished doctoral dissertation, Brandeis University, Waltham, MA.

Friedman, M., Thoresen, C. E., Gill, J. J., Powell, L. H., Ulmer, D., Thompson, L., Price, V. A., Rabin, D. D., Breall, W. W., Dixon, T., Levy, R., & Bourg, E. (1986). Alteration of Type A behavior and its effect on cardiac recurrences in post myocardial infarction patients: Summary results of the recurrent coronary prevention project. *American Heart Journal, 112,* 653-665.

Fullerton, C. S., Yates, B. T., & Goodrich, W. (1990). Therapist gender, client gender, and therapist experience relate to therapeutic improvement with adolescents. In S. C. Feinstein (Ed.), *Adolescent psychiatry* (Vol. 17). Chicago: University of Chicago Press.

Goldberg, D. (1991). Cost-effectiveness studies in the treatment of schizophrenia: A review. *Schizophrenia Bulletin, 17,* 453-459.

Gottman, J. M., & Leiblum, S. R. (1974). *How to do psychotherapy and how to evaluate it.* New York: Holt, Rinehart & Winston.

Gray, C. A., & Shields, J. J. (1992). The development of an instrument to measure the psychological response to separation and divorce. *Journal of Divorce & Remarriage, 17*(1), 43-56.

Guba, E. G., & Lincoln, Y. S. (1989). *Fourth generation evaluation.* Newbury Park, CA: Sage.

Haaga, D. A., Dyck, M. J., & Ernst, D. (1991). Empirical status of cognitive theory of depression. *Psychological Bulletin, 110,* 215-236.

Häfner, H., & Wolfram, H. (1991). Evaluating effectiveness and cost of community care for schizophrenia patients. *Schizophrenia Bulletin, 17,* 441-451.

Halfon, N. (1990). *Health and mental health service utilization by children in foster care in California.* Berkeley: University of California, California Policy Seminar. (ERIC Clearinghouse No. PS 020 536)

Harwood, H. J., Hubbard, R. L., Collins, J. J., & Rachal, J. V. (1988). The costs of crime and the benefits of drug abuse treatment: A cost-benefit analysis using TOPS data. In C. G. Leukefeld & F. M. Tims (Eds.), *Compulsory treatment of drug abuse: Research and clinical practice* (pp. 209-235) (Research Monograph 86). Rockville, MD: National Institute on Drug Abuse.

Hayes, L. M., & Rowan, J. R. (1988). *Training curriculum on suicide detection and prevention in jail and lock-ups.* Alexandria, VA: National Center on Institutions and Alternatives.

Hillier, F. S., & Lieberman, G. J. (1974). *Operations research* (2nd ed.). San Francisco: Holden-Day.

Jaeger, R. M. (1984). *Sampling in education and the social sciences.* New York: Longman.

James, L. R., Mulaik, S. A., & Brett, J. M. (1982). *Causal analysis: Assumptions, models, and data.* Beverly Hills, CA: Sage.

Jarrett, R. B., & Nelson, R. O. (1987). Mechanisms of change in cognitive therapy of depression. *Behavior Therapy, 18,* 227-241.

Jayaratne, S., & Levy, R. L. (1979). *Empirical clinical practice.* New York: Columbia University Press.

Johnson, S. M., & Bolstad, O. D. (1973). Methodological issues in naturalistic observation: Some problems and solutions for field research. In L. A. Hamerlynck, L. C. Handy, & E. J. Mash (Eds.), *Behavior change: Methodology, concepts, and practice* (pp. 7-68). Champaign, IL: Research Press.

Jones, K. R., & Vischi, T. R. (1979). Impact of alcohol, drug abuse, and mental health treatment on medical care utilization: A review of the research literature. *Medical Care, 17*(Suppl.), 1-82.

Jorgensen, D. L. (1989). *Participant observation: A methodology for human studies* (Applied Social Research Methods Series, Vol. 15). Newbury Park, CA: Sage.

Jung, C. G. (1965). *Memories, dreams, reflections.* New York: Vintage.

Katona, G. (1975). *Psychological economics.* New York: Elsevier.

Kazdin, A. E. (1982). *Single-case research designs: Methods for clinical and applied settings.* New York: Oxford University Press.

Kazdin, A. E. (1992). *Research design in clinical psychology* (2nd ed.). New York: Macmillan.

Kazdin, A. E. (1993). Evaluation in clinical practice: Clinically sensitive and systematic methods of treatment delivery. *Behavior Therapy, 24*(1), 11-45.

Kendall, M. G. (Ed.). (1971). *Cost-benefit analysis.* New York: Elsevier.

Kessler, L. G. (Ed.). (1981). *Operations research and the mental health service system: Vol. 1. Report of the Ad Hoc Advisory Group* (Series HN No. 1, DHHS Publication No. ADM 80-1018). Rockville, MD: National Institute of Mental Health, Division of Biometry and Epidemiology.

Kiresuk, T. J., & Lund, S. H. (1978). Goal attainment scaling. In C. C. Attkisson, W. A. Hargreaves, & M. J. Horowitz (Eds.), *Evaluation of human service programs* (pp. 341-370). New York: Academic Press.

Kirigen, K. A., Braukmann, C. J., Atwater, J., & Wolf, M. M. (1977). *A consumer and outcome evaluation of community group homes for juvenile offenders: A comparison of trained and untrained child-care staff.* Paper presented at the meeting of the National Conference on Criminal Justice Evaluation, Washington, DC.

Kohler, P. D. (1993). *Serving students with disabilities in postsecondary education settings: A conceptual framework of program outcomes.* Unpublished doctoral dissertation, University of Illinois at Urbana-Champaign.

Krantz, D. H., & Tversky, A. (1971). Conjoint-measurement analysis of composition rules in psychology. *Psychological Review, 78,* 151-169.

Kuhl, J. (1985). From cognition to behavior: Perspectives for future research on action control. In J. Kuhl & J. Beckmann (Eds.), *Action control from cognition to behavior.* New York: Springer-Verlag.

Kuhn, A. A. (1974). *The logic of social systems.* San Francisco: Jossey-Bass.

Lally, J. R., Mangione, P. L., & Honig, A. S. (1988). The Syracuse University Family Development Research Project: Long-range impact of an early intervention with low-income children and their families. In D. R. Powell (Ed.), *Annual advances in applied developmental psychology: Vol. 3. Parent education as early childhood* intervention: *Emerging directions in theory, research, and practice* (pp. 79-104). Norwood, NJ: Ablex.

Lamiell, J. T. (1981). Toward an idiothetic psychology of personality. *American Psychologist, 36,* 276-289.

Langer, E. J., & Abelson, R. P. (1974). A patient by any other name . . . : Clinical group differences in labeling bias. *Journal of Consulting and Clinical Psychology, 42*(1), 4-9.

Lasky, J. J., Hover, C. L., Smith, P. A., Bostian, D. W., Duffendach, S. C., & Nord, C. L. (1959). Post-hospital adjustment as predicted by psychiatric patients and their staff. *Journal of Consulting Psychology, 23,* 213-218.

Lavrakas, P. J. (1993). *Telephone survey methods: Sampling, selection, and supervision* (2nd ed., Applied Social Research Methods Series, Vol. 7). Newbury Park, CA: Sage.

Levin, H. M. (1983). *Cost-effectiveness.* Beverly Hills, CA: Sage.

Lewis, D. R., Johnson, D. R., Chen, T. H., & Erickson, R. N. (1992). The use and reporting of benefit-cost analyses by state vocational rehabilitation agencies. *Evaluation Review, 16,* 266-287.

Linehan, M. M., & Wagner, A. W. (1990). Dialectical behavior therapy: A feminist-behavioral treatment of borderline personality disorder. *The Behavior Therapist, 13*(1), 9-14.

Lipsey, M. W. (1993). Theory as method: Small theories of treatments. In L. B. Sechrest & A. G. Scott (Eds.), *Understanding causes and generalizing about them* (New Directions for Program Evaluation, No. 57, pp. 5-38). San Francisco: Jossey-Bass.

Longman, D. R. (1978). *Distribution cost analysis.* New York: Arno. (Original work published in 1941)

Longo, D. J., Clum, G. A., & Yaeger, N. J. (1988). Psychosocial treatment of recurrent genital herpes. *Journal of Consulting and Clinical Psychology, 56*(1), 61-66.

Louviere, J. J. (1988). *Analyzing decision making: Metric conjoint analysis.* Newbury Park, CA: Sage.

Mahoney, M. J. (1991). *Human change processes: The scientific foundations of psychotherapy.* New York: Basic Books.

Manuso, J. (1978). Testimony to the President's Commission on Mental Health, Panel on Cost and Financing. *Report of the President's Commission on Mental Health: Appendix* (Vol. 2, p. 512). Washington, DC: Government Printing Office.

Manuso, J. (1981). Psychological services and health enhancement: A corporate model. In A. Broskowski, E. Marks, & S. H. Budman (Eds.), *Linking health and mental health* (pp. 137-158). Beverly Hills, CA: Sage.

Marcuse, H. (1964). *One dimensional man.* Boston: Beacon.

McDowell, C. L. (1992). Standardized tests and program evaluation: Inappropriate measures in critical times. In A. M. Madison (Ed.), *Minority issues in program evaluation* (New Directions in Program Evaluation, No. 53, pp. 45-54). San Francisco: Jossey-Bass.

McGuire, T. G. (1991). Measuring the economic costs of schizophrenia. *Schizophrenia Bulletin, 17,* 375-394.

McLellan, A. T., Luborsky, L., Cacciola, M., Griffith, B., Evans, F., Barr, H., & O'Brien, C. (1985). New data from the Addiction Severity Index. *Journal of Nervous and Mental Disease, 173,* 412-423.

McLellan, A. T., Luborsky, L., Cacciola, M., Griffith, B., McGahan, P., & O'Brien, C. P. (1985). *Guide to the Addiction Severity Index.* Washington, DC: Government Printing Office.

McLellan, A. T., Luborsky, L., Woody, G. E., & O'Brien, C. P. (1980). An improved diagnostic evaluation instrument for substance abuse patients: The Addiction Severity Index. *Journal of Nervous and Mental Disease, 168*(1), 26-33.

Miller, G. A. (1988). *The Substance Abuse Subtle Screening Inventory manual.* Spencer, IN: Spencer Evening World.

Mischel, W. (1965). Predicting the success of Peace Corps volunteers in Nigeria. *Journal of Personality and Social Psychology, 1,* 510-517.

Mishan, E. J. (1988). *Cost-benefit analysis: An informal introduction* (4th ed.). London: Unwin Hyman.

Molloy, J. P. (1992). *Development and evaluation of the New Jersey network of Oxford Houses* (Report to the State of New Jersey Department of Health, Division of Alcoholism and Substance Abuse, Grant No. 92-632-ADA). Silver Spring, MD: Oxford House.

Newman, F. L., & Sorensen, J. E. (1985). *Integrated clinical and fiscal management in mental health: A guidebook.* Norwood, NJ: Ablex.

Office of Technology Assessment. (1980). *The implications of cost-effectiveness analysis of medical technology.* Washington, DC: Author, U.S. Congress.

Onken, L. S., & Blaine, J. D. (Eds.). (1990). *Psychotherapy and counseling in treatment of drug abuse* (NIDA Research Monograph No. 104). Rockville, MD: National Institute on Drug Abuse.

Overall, J. E., & Woodward, J. A. (1977). Nonrandom assignment and the analysis of covariance. *Psychological Bulletin, 84,* 588-594.

Pallak, M. S., Cummings, N. A., Dorken, H., & Henke, C. J. (1994). Medical costs, Medicaid, and managed mental health treatment: The Hawaii study. *Managed Care Quarterly, 2*(1), 64-70.

Parloff, M. B. (1986). Placebo controls in psychotherapy research: A sine qua non or a placebo for research problems? *Journal of Consulting and Clinical Psychology, 54,* 79-87.

Patterson, G. R., Ray, R. S., Shaw, D. A., & Cobb, T. A. (1969). *A manual for coding of family interactions.* New York: Microfiche Publications.

Patterson, G. R., Reid, J. B., Jones, R. R., & Conger, R. E. (1975). *A social learning approach to family intervention.* Eugene, OR: Castalia.

Peterson, R. D. (1986). The anatomy of cost-effectiveness analysis. *Evaluation Review, 10,* 29-44.

Pires, S. A. (1990). *Sizing components of care: An approach to determining the size and cost of service components in a system of care for children and adolescents with serious emotional disturbances.* Washington, DC: Georgetown University Hospital, CASSP Technical Assistance Center, Child Development Center. (ERIC Clearinghouse No. EC 300 148)

Pirrong, G. D. (1993, February). As easy as ABC: Using activity based costing in service industries. *National Public Accountant,* pp. 22-26.

Posavac, E. J., & Carey, R. G. (1989). *Program evaluation: Methods and case studies* (3rd ed.). Englewood Cliffs, NJ: Prentice-Hall.

Prochaska, J. O., DiClemente, C. C., & Norcross, J. C. (1992). In search of how people change: Applications to addictive behaviors. *American Psychologist, 47,* 1102-1114.

Prochaska, J. O., Velicer, W. F., Rossi, J. S., Goldstein, M. G., Marcus, B. H., Rakowski, W., Fiore, C., Harlow, L. L., Redding, C. A., Rosenbloom, D., & Rossi, S. R. (1994). Stages of change and decisional balance for 12 problem behaviors. *Health Psychology, 13,* 39-46.

Rea, L. M. (1992). *Designing and conducting survey research: A comprehensive guide.* San Francisco: Jossey-Bass.

Reynolds, R. V. (1987). Computer-automated service delivery: A primer. *The Behavior Therapist, 10,* 115-120.

Richman, G. S., Riordan, M. R., Reiss, M. L., Pyles, D. A., & Bailey, J. S. (1988). The effects of self-monitoring and supervisor feedback on staff performance in a residential setting. *Journal of Applied Behavior Analysis, 21,* 401-409.

Robins, E., Murphy, G. E., & Wilkinson, R. H., Jr. (1959). Some clinical considerations in the prevention of suicide based on a study of 134 successful suicides. *American Journal of Public Health, 235,* 2105-2109.

Robinson, F. P. (1970). *Effective study* (4th ed.). New York: Harper & Row.

Rog, D. J. (1985). *A methodological analysis of evaluability assessment.* Master's thesis, Vanderbilt University, Nashville, TN.

Rossi, P. H., & Chen, H. (Eds.). (1992). *Using theory to improve program and policy evaluation* (Contributions in Political Sciences Series, No. 290). Westport, CT: Greenwood.

Rounsaville, B. J., Chevron, E. S., Prusoff, B. A., Elkin, I., Imber, S., Stosky, S., & Watkins, J. (1986). The relation between specific and general dimensions of the psychotherapy process in interpersonal psychotherapy of depression. *Journal of Consulting and Clinical Psychology, 55,* 379-394.

Schweinhart, L. J., Barnes, H. V., & Weikart, D. P. (Eds.). (1993). *Significant benefits: The High/Scope Perry Preschool Study through age 27.* Ypsilanti, MI: High/Scope.

Siegert, F. A., & Yates, B. T. (1980). Cost-effectiveness of individual in-office, individual in-home, and group delivery systems for behavioral child-management. *Evaluation & the Health Professions, 3*(2), 123-152.

Silkman, R., Kelley, J. M., & Wolf, W. C. (1983). An evaluation of two preemployment services: Impact on employment and earnings of disadvantaged youths. *Evaluation Review, 7,* 467-496.

Silverstein, A. (1988). An Aristotelian resolution of the idiographic versus nomothetic tradition. *American Psychologist, 43,* 425-430.

Sloane, R. B., Staples, F. R., Cristol, A. H., Yorkston, N. J., & Whipple, K. (1975). *Psychotherapy versus behavior therapy.* Cambridge, MA: Harvard University Press.

Smith, M. L., Glass, G. V., & Miller, T. I. (1980). *The benefits of psychotherapy.* Baltimore: Johns Hopkins University Press.

Sorensen, J. E., & Hanbery, G. W. (1979). *Using financial management in mental health organizations.* Rockville, MD: National Institute of Mental Health.

Sorensen, J. E., & Phipps, D. W. (1975). *Cost-finding and rate-setting for community mental health centers* (DHEW Publication No. ADM 76-291). Washington, DC: Government Printing Office.

Spitzer, R. L., Gibbon, M., & Endicott, J. (1975). Global Assessment Scale. In W. A. Hargreaves, C. C. Attkisson, L. M. Siegel, M. H. McIntyre, & J. E. Sorensen (Eds.), *Resource materials for community mental health program evaluation* (DHEW Publication No. ADM 75-222). Rockville, MD: National Institute of Mental Health.

Steiger, J. H. (1989). *EzPATH: A supplementary module for SYSTAT and SYGRAPH.* Evanston, IL: SYSTAT.

Stone, A. A., Cox, D. S., Valdimarsdottir, H., Jandorf, L., & Neale, J. M. (1987). Evidence that secretory IgA antibody is associated with daily mood. *Journal of Personality and Social Psychology, 52,* 988-993.

Strupp, H. H., & Hadley, S. W. (1979). Specific versus nonspecific factors in psychotherapy: A controlled study of outcome. *Archives of General Psychiatry, 36,* 1125-1146.

Taylor, J. A. (1953). A personality scale of manifest anxiety. *Journal of Abnormal and Social Psychology, 48,* 285-290.

Teegarden, L. A., & Burns, G. L. (1993). Construct validity of the Sutter-Eyberg Student Behavior Inventory: Relation between teacher perception of disruptive behavior and direct observation of problem classroom behavior over a seven month interval. *Child and Family Behavior Therapy, 15*(1), 43-58.

Thomas, J. A. (1971). *The productive school: A systems analysis approach to educational administration.* New York: John Wiley.

Thompson, M. S. (1980). *Benefit-cost analysis for program evaluation.* Beverly Hills, CA: Sage.

Trochim, M. K. (1989). An introduction to concept mapping for planning and evaluation. *Evaluation and Program Planning, 12,* 1-16.

Trochim, M. K., & Linton, R. (1986). Conceptualization for planning and evaluation. *Evaluation and Program Planning, 9,* 289-308.

Turner, R. A., Irwin, C. E., Jr., Tschann, J. M., & Millstein, S. G. (1993). Autonomy, relatedness, and the initiation of health risk behaviors in early adolescence. *Health Psychology, 12,* 200-208.

Weisbrod, B. A. (1983). A guide to benefit-cost analysis, as seen through a controlled experiment in treating the mentally ill. *Journal of Health Politics, Policy, and Law, 8,* 808-845.

Wholey, J. S. (1983). *Evaluation and effective public management.* Boston: Little, Brown.

Wholey, J. S. (1987a). Evaluability assessment: Developing program theory. In L. Bickman (Ed.), *Using program theory in evaluation* (New Directions for Program Evaluation, No. 33, pp. 77-92). San Francisco: Jossey-Bass.

Wholey, J. S. (Ed.). (1987b). *Organizational excellence: Stimulating quality and communicating value.* New York: Free Press.

Willette, R. E. (1989). Drug testing programs. In *Urine testing for drugs of abuse* (DHHS Publication No. ADM 87-1481). Rockville, MD: National Institute on Drug Abuse.

Williams, D. V., & Yates, B. T. (1993, April 16). *The predictive value of expectancies of self-efficacy, compliance, outcome, and difficulty on weight reduction.* Paper presented at the meeting of the Eastern Psychological Association, Crystal City, VA.

Yates, B. T. (1975). *Student involvement in Learning House.* Stanford, CA: Stanford University, Department of Psychology.

Yates, B. T. (1978). Improving the cost-effectiveness of obesity programs: Reducing the cost per pound. *International Journal of Obesity, 2,* 249-266.

Yates, B. T. (1980a). Benefits and costs of community-academia interaction in a paraprofessional training course. *Teaching of Psychology, 7*(1), 8-12.

Yates, B. T. (1980b). *Improving effectiveness and reducing costs in mental health.* Springfield, IL: Charles C Thomas.

Yates, B. T. (1980c). Survey comparison of success, morbidity, mortality, fees, and psychological benefits and costs of 3,146 patients receiving jejunoileal or gastric bypass. *American Journal of Clinical Nutrition, 33,* 518-522.

Yates, B. T. (1980d). The theory and practice of cost-utility, cost-effectiveness, and cost-benefit analysis in behavioral medicine: Toward delivering more health care for less money. In J. M. Ferguson & C. B. Taylor (Eds.), *The comprehensive handbook of behavioral medicine, Vol. 3: Extended applications and issues* (pp. 165-205). New York: SP Medical & Scientific.

Yates, B. T. (1985). *Self-management: The science and art of helping yourself.* Belmont, CA: Wadsworth.

Yates, B. T. (1986a). *Applications in self-management.* Belmont, CA: Wadsworth.

Yates, B. T. (1986b). Economics of suicide: Toward cost-effectiveness and cost-benefit analysis of suicide prevention. In R. Cross (Ed.), *Non-natural death: Coming to terms with suicide, euthanasia, withholding or withdrawing treatment.* Denver, CO: Rose Medical Center.

Yates, B. T. (1987). Cognitive vs. diet vs. exercise components in obesity bibliotherapy: Effectiveness as a function of psychological benefits versus psychological costs. *The Southern Psychologist, 3*(1), 35-40.

Yates, B. T. (1994). Toward the incorporation of costs, cost-effectiveness analysis, and cost-benefit analysis into clinical research. *Journal of Consulting and Clinical Psychology, 62,* 729-736.

Yates, B. T. (1995). Cost-effectiveness analysis, cost-benefit analysis, and beyond: Evolving models for the scientist-manager-practitioner. *Clinical Psychology: Science and Practice, 2,* 385-398.

Yates, B. T., Besteman, K. J., Filipczak, J., & Greenfield, L. (1993). *Assessing the costs of substance abuse services, administration, and research: Toward a methodology of measuring the value of resources consumed.* Unpublished manuscript.

Yates, B. T., & Filipczak, J. A. (1989, April 14). *Cost → process → outcome analysis: Management information systems for quality assurance and cost analysis.* Paper presented at the Tenth International Conference of the Young Adult Institute, New York.

Yates, B. T., Haven, W. G., & Thoresen, C. E. (1979). Cost-effectiveness analysis at Learning House: How much change for how much money? In J. S. Stumphauzer (Ed.), *Progress in behavior therapy with delinquents.* Springfield, IL: Charles C Thomas.

Yates, B. T., & Hoage, C. M. (1982). Mnemonic distortion following behavior observation: Interactions of negative versus positive behavior valence, diagnostic label, and relative behavior frequency. *Cognitive Therapy and Research, 6,* 213-217.

Yates, B. T., & Newman, F. L. (1980a). Approaches to cost-effectiveness analysis and cost-benefit analysis of psychotherapy. In G. VandenBos (Ed.), *Psychotherapy: Practice, research, policy.* Beverly Hills, CA: Sage.

Yates, B. T., & Newman, F. L. (1980b). Findings of cost-effectiveness and cost-benefit analyses of psychotherapy. In G. VandenBos (Ed.), *Psychotherapy: Practice, research, policy.* Beverly Hills, CA: Sage.

Yates, B. T., Yokley, J. M., & Thomas, J. V. (1994). Cost-benefit analysis of six alternative payment incentives for child therapists. *Journal of Consulting and Clinical Psychology, 62,* 627-635.

Young, D. W. (1988, March). Cost accounting and cost comparisons: Methodological issues and their policy and management implications. *Accounting Horizons,* 67-76.

Zuardi, A. W., Loureiro, S. R., & Rodrigues, C. R. (1995). Reliability, validity and factorial dimensions of the Interactive Observation Scale for Psychiatric Inpatients. *Acta Psychiatrica Scandinavica, 91,* 247.

Index

About the Author

Brian T. Yates received his PhD in psychology from Stanford University in 1976. He is a tenured Associate Professor in the Department of Psychology of the College of Arts and Sciences at American University in Washington, DC, where he has worked since 1976. *Analyzing Costs, Procedures, Processes, and Outcomes* is his fifth book and his first with Sage. His book, *Improving Effectiveness and Reducing Costs in Mental Health,* published in 1980, laid the ground work for the present integration of psychological decision-making strategies and quasi-experimental design with the concepts and methods adapted from economics and operations research. His other books include a practical guide to doing the dissertation and two texts on self-management.

Dr. Yates has published over 50 articles and book chapters. Some are basic research studies in psychology: most apply cost-effectiveness or cost-benefit analysis to the systematic evaluation and improvement of human services. This book presents his complete model of Cost → Procedure → Process → Outcome Analysis (CPPOA) developed over two decades of consulting with a variety of public and private organizations specializing in service and research. He has conducted CPPOA for service enterprises and research initiatives in the treatment of heroin and cocaine addiction, foster programs for youth, intermediate care facilities for mentally retarded adults, suicide prevention, psychiatric inpatient treatment for schizophrenic adolescents, and prevention of alcohol, tobacco, and other substance abuse. These remain his current interests along with assessment and minimization of HIV risk behaviors in young adults.

APPLIED SOCIAL RESEARCH
METHODS SERIES

Series Editors
LEONARD BICKMAN, Peabody College, Vanderbilt University, Nashville
DEBRA J. ROG, Vanderbilt University, Washington, DC

Other volumes in this series are listed on the series page